A DETAILED BOOK
ON THE ART OF SELLING
PERSONAL TRAINING

Written by Ron Thatcher

Edited by Jeff Evans and Chad McCleary

Marketed by R.T. Consulting

Book design, typesetting: Roy Diment VRG
www.members.shaw.ca/vrg

Note for Librarians: A cataloguing record for this book is available from Library and Archives Canada at www.collectionscanada.ca/amicus/index-e.html
ISBN 1-4120-7087-2

PUBLISHING™

Offices in Canada, USA, Ireland and UK
This book was published *on-demand* in cooperation with Trafford Publishing. On-demand publishing is a unique process and service of making a book available for retail sale to the public taking advantage of on-demand manufacturing and Internet marketing. On-demand publishing includes promotions, retail sales, manufacturing, order fulfilment, accounting and collecting royalties on behalf of the author.

Book sales for North America and international:
Trafford Publishing, 6E–2333 Government St.,
Victoria, BC v8t 4p4 CANADA
phone 250 383 6864 (toll-free 1 888 232 4444)
fax 250 383 6804; email to orders@trafford.com
Book sales in Europe:
Trafford Publishing (uk) Limited, 9 Park End Street, 2nd Floor
Oxford, UK ox1 1hh UNITED KINGDOM
phone 44 (0)1865 722 113 (local rate 0845 230 9601)
facsimile 44 (0)1865 722 868; info.uk@trafford.com
Order online at:
trafford.com/05-1998

10 9 8 7 6 5 4 3 2

Contents

This book is dedicated to:

Spencer Belideau for teaching me how to sell personal training.
John Caraccio for giving me the opportunity to offer
my personal training system in Taiwan.

CHAPTER 1

INTRODUCTION

Welcome to ***Selling Personal Training!!!*** This book is going to offer the personal trainer or fitness professional an amazing opportunity to understand and master the business side of personal training. If you are ready to stop struggling and start producing, then get ready to enjoy the first book that has ever been written using the actual techniques coveted by the top personal trainers in the fitness industry.

This book will introduce you to the techniques that have built some of the largest, most successful training programs throughout the world. The fitness industry's top producers have kept these proven techniques secret for decades. The material contained within this book has been tested, tried and retested before being implemented to produce outstanding financial success. Not only will you get the inside track on how to get the most out of a career as a certified personal trainer, but you will also learn that establishing and maintaining a quality client list is a crucial aspect of your long-term success.

One unavoidable aspect of helping people to get results is collecting money, that is, if you are unable to sell your service, is it likely that you will be able to continue to give it away? I mean, what are you going to say the next time the club owner asks you, "How much personal training did you sell last month?" or "How many clients do you have resigning this week?" These are tough issues that nobody wants to write about or face up to. Let's be honest and to the point. **Selling is hard!** It is much easier to just not ask.

The bottom line is that it is much easier if you have been properly trained on how and when to propose the sale of a personal training package. The anxiety that you are experiencing over asking for money will start to subside after reading this book. I know what you are thinking, "I am a personal trainer, not a salesman." Well, I have thought about this a lot and the simple fact of the matter is that you are a counselor, teacher, motivator, coach and sometimes even psychiatrist, but you are a salesman. However, not all personal trainers are working for commission, some are actually paid an hourly rate. If you are one of the "fortunate" ones working for a base salary, I am quite certain that it isn't very substantial.

Operationally, your first days working as a personal trainer will consist of many long hours of self-education in relation to product knowledge. Sooner or later, you will begin to feel the pressure of the person who is in charge of driving revenue for your particular facility. Whether it's the stress from receiving small paychecks, or the pressure from the person in charge of production in your club, you will feel that it is time to learn how to produce an income from your efforts. Your routine will no doubt start where most personal training careers start and you will find yourself taking new members through an orientation workout. Even if your club does not offer this type of opportunity and you are responsible for creating your own sales opportunities, the fact remains the same. The best way to consistently produce new clients is to offer some sort of orientation or free introductory program. Success as a personal trainer is a derivative of converting these introductory "one time" workouts into long-term one-on-one personal training clients. If you study the scripts, practicing methods and closing techniques in this book you will have more success than you ever dreamed possible. Soon, the road to financial success as a personal trainer will become clear and more enjoyable.

As an active health club operator, I find that I spend a good portion of my time trying to improve the fitness business as a whole. In recent times the health club industry has been criticized for using questionable business practices. This criticism always seems to center around the shortcomings of the selling process. In my opinion, the focus of this criticism should not be on the selling process. The shortcomings that I have recognized stem from the rapid growth of the fitness industry as a whole. This, coupled with a lack of systematic education, as well as the lack of long term employment opportunities are the true issues that plague the fitness industry. I have set out not only to increase investor support but also to improve and standardize training. I have tried to develop a process from which club owners, managers and employees can systematically develop a long-term healthy plan for investors, members and communities. My systems, like the ones used in my first book *Fitness Memberships and Money* are meant to be internalized so they can be practiced and utilized although they should merely act as a foundation upon which one should build and improve according to individual needs. I wrote this book with that philosophy in mind. I wrote this book for all the personal trainers that fear going to work at a job they love because they have to sell. I wrote this book to compensate for the certification programs that are misleading young students in regards to the day-to-day life as a personal trainer. I wrote this book for all the members that say thank you for changing my life. Thank you for convincing me to make a decision today.

Chapter 2

THE DOCTOR

 Alvin Stein III had spent much of his life studying to be a doctor. He had devoted his youth learning about the complicated and diverse systems of the human body. He learned all the technical terms that were important in practicing medicine. Alvin's father and grandfather were both doctors. His father taught him well; ensuring that his son learned everything required of an upcoming successful physician. His father always taught him "that we don't heal books, we heal people," this would become more prevalent in the future. Alvin was encouraged to become involved in sports and became a good all-around athlete at a young age. He was on the swimming team and the basketball team, earning an award for being the most improved swimmer in his senior year. Alvin received a partial scholarship as a student athlete and he was off to Stanford to begin his college education. He was excited about going to college, especially as he was going to an even more prestigious school than that of his father. He was very enthusiastic about becoming a medical doctor and was excited by the thought of saving a person's life. He was a diligent and hard working student who had joined the swimming team as a requirement of his scholarship, and had gone on to become a letterman with the Varsity Swimming Team. His college years passed quickly and he was soon applying for medical school. His participation in athletics helped him mentally and emotionally in areas that left his peers challenged and at times struggling. Understanding the theory was an easy task for some of them, however attempting to utilize and demonstrate their knowledge in a practical manner was often too difficult. Many of the med-students failed to apply this knowledge and information while working on a cadaver. Alvin reflected on what his dad had once said and stated, "My dad was right! We don't heal books, many of the things that we learned in our books are actually very different once you study the anatomy of the human body." As medical school came to an end, Alvin was given the opportunity to complete his internship in Minnesota at the prestigious Mayo Clinic. Things were going well and the time for Alvin to actually commence his medical career was just around the corner! Alvin moved away from his home in sunny California to complete his studies as an intern. Life was vastly different in Minnesota and he had a difficult time adjusting to the cold weather and the grueling 24-hour shifts. He also had his first feelings of self-doubt in this challenging environment filled with sickness and death. Alvin questioned whether he was capable of achieving his goal of becoming a doctor and called his father weekly for moral support and advice. He informed him of his difficulties and asked him if his internship experience had been similar. Alvin's father offered understanding and encouraged him to be strong, "I completed my internship during a tour in the Vietnam War and it was atrocious. When I came back, being a doctor and running my own clinic was a breeze." He also reminded his son that the internship was designed to be a test. Once the test was over his life of being a doctor would be a breeze as well. Alvin had always wanted to learn the ropes from his dedicated dad. He soon completed his internship and was ready to start working in his father's busy clinic. Alvin was doing well and business was thriving. However, soon after a distressing problem arose. The insurance companies were changing their policies, leaving older patients with insufficient coverage for adequate health care. Matters worsened when an elderly patient that Alvin had been treating passed away leaving his widow with medical bills and rejected insurance. This was starting to put serious pressure on the business and on Alvin's life. He began dreading work and the day soon came when he had to tell his father that was going to leave the medical field. His father said, "Son, I have been waiting for this day to come. I had hoped it wouldn't, but the day is here. I have something special for you. Your Grandfather said this was an area of weakness in his profession. You see your Grandfather was a genuine-hearted man and back in those days people were poor. They would die because they couldn't afford to pay the doctor. Your grandfather gave away so much free medical care that he himself went bankrupt. This book was given to your grandfather and it was an instrumental part of your Grandfather's ability to recover from financial ruin. It was given to your grandfather from a teacher at Harvard. The book was never published and it was really made up from secret techniques used by Harvard doctors who had run very successful clinics.

The book mainly focused on a different side of being a doctor. The cover of the book had only two words on it simply reading, 'Selling Medicine.' The book was not only given to your grandfather but it was also given to another doctor who was in your same situation. The book was given to a talented doctor who had an incredible talent to cure the sick and was ready to give up. This book has a reputation for being the savior of many generations of doctors." As Alvin's father pulled the book from an old dusty box, he explained that he searched high and low to retrieve the book because he knew that it had meant so much to his father. "I also knew that someday it just might come in handy. Now my son, I give the book to you. May you let the age-old words encompass the art of being a master of our trade. We must thank the hard-won work of those who have come before us, while also challenging and emulating their success in all areas." As Alvin opened the book, he noticed the penciled in writing. "My son this is a true story and it is to remind you that every case is as different in nature as the ailment from which it has come, some times the heart is the only medicine needed."

(I am not talking about the patients; this book is to heal the Doctor!)

" A Red Cross soldier"

One day, a Red Cross soldier who was selling anything in his bag from door to door to pay his way back over the border, found he had only one thin dime left. You see his plane had crash-landed during a peace mission, and he was very hungry.

He decided he would ask for a meal at the next house. However, he lost his nerve when a lovely young woman opened the door. Instead of a meal, he asked for a drink of water.

She thought he looked hungry, so she brought him a large bowl of soup. He ate it slowly, and then asked, "How much do I owe you?"

You don't owe me anything," she replied. "Mother has taught us never to accept pay for a kindness."

He said, "Then I thank you from my heart."

As Alvin Stein left that house, he not only felt stronger physically, but his faith in man was stronger. He had been ready to give up and quit. Many year's later, that same young woman became critically ill.

The local doctors were baffled. They finally sent her to the big city, where they called in specialists to study her rare disease. Dr. Alvin Stein was called in for the consultation. When he heard the name of the town she came from, a strange light filled his eyes. Immediately, he rose and went down the hall to her room.

Dressed in his doctor's gown, he went in to see her. He recognized her at once. He went back to the consultation room and was determined to do his best to save her life. From that day, he gave special attention to her case. After a long struggle, the battle was won.

Dr. Stein requested the business office to pass the final bill to him for approval. He looked at it, and then wrote something on the edge and the bill was sent to her room. She feared to open it, for she was sure it would take the rest of her life to pay this bill.

Finally she looked, and something caught her attention on the side of the bill. She then read these words...

"Paid in full with one bowl of soup"

(Signed) Dr. Alvin Stein.

Tears of joy flooded her eyes as her happy heart prayed: "Thank You, God, that your love has spread broad through human hearts and hands."

You should remember this story my son! This book was given to me from a friend to help me cope with my own personal fear of dealing with the business side of being a doctor. You must trust your heart and remember not every case is the same.

Your father,

Alvin Stein the first

This was written in pencil by his own hand in the front of your Grandfathers book!

"Dad are you saying that he gave this book to you?" "You were the doctor that was ready to give up, and Grandpa gave the book to you?" "WHAT IS THE BOOK REALLY ABOUT?" "It will teach you how to ask for money and make a living as a doctor!"

"My son, there are three different kinds of doctors in this world; the first are the ones that own clinics, they are good businessmen and they make the most money. The second are the doctors that work for the hospitals, they are the ones that don't like dealing with the business side so they let the hospitals deal with most of it, but they still get some of the patients coming back to them. The third is the doctor like the ones that do research and teach at schools, they hate the business side so much that they didn't even talk about *it* for the entire 12 years that they had spent at medical school. The business end of being a doctor brings out their worst fears and most of them were never willing to face those fears head on by taking up the challenge. Son, in all jobs there will be some parts that you may not like!" "SOME PEOPLE WILL FOLD UP TENT AND QUIT, THE STEINS FOCUS!"

Chapter 3

HOW THE SYSTEM WORKS

The system operates through constant repetition. It relies on systematic improvement of skills through practice. The system works with proven techniques to be used and referenced. Different areas of your arsenal must be used over and over in "real life" (role playing) situations until they are perfected. The system must be used and not merely read. When teaching systems I get my staff to practice role-playing situations as opposed to me standing up and talking to them. This way I can be certain that they have learned the material, that they know how to use the scripts and that they are ready to deal with clients. I then make them present in front of a large group or the staff. If they can perform in front of the entire sales team, they can present it to a member or several potential clients.

I also make the staff accountable to have the scripts memorized by a certain date. If they do not have them memorized, then I make them present it to me every day until they do. Remember, the accountability factor is the key to managing the health club and yourself simultaneously. Nothing will be accomplished without accountability. If you are a self-starter this may be easy for you. If you are not this task may take a little more time. You have to turn any system that you use in the health club into a habit. Once something is a habit, it becomes easier, enabling you to enjoy it more. The goals you set for yourself must be as important as the ones you set for your clients. You must approach them in the same manner: one step at a time.

If you are a new personal trainer the first thing you must do is memorize the sale presentation scripts word for word.

When small business health clubs transformed into big business, investors desired standardized systems. This is when I came into the picture. I worked for one of the largest health club companies in California. We had just reached the 20-club milestone and we had received a large injection of cash to expand our company even further. Personal training had just become something that was offered to our members and I had the unique opportunity to work in a club that had been allocated for the pilot program. A pilot program is where you take a new system and you test it and try it in one particular location. Once you have taken a core system and developed it into something that works, you then work out the bugs and problems and finally you implement your system into the rest of the organization. Programs like these are developed with very careful planning and implemented under the watchful supervision of company management. The teams chosen for this difficult task were handpicked to deliver optimum results. As the systems for selling personal training was developed, I had the opportunity to work as a membership counselor and was able to help bring this incredible new program to the front lines. We were a fantastic group of highly motivated individuals. We had drank the potion and bought in to the company systems, 110%. We believed that we were part of something that was going to change the industry and that we could make a difference in the lives of our personal training clients. The system that we created took several months and underwent many transformations before it became the product that most health club companies use today. Thousands of people have benefited from the results and the systems that were created during this pilot program. It is amazing the kind of energy you can create from a group of individuals that believe and work toward achieving a common goal. I believe that my ability to build successful teams has come from my ability to duplicate this atmosphere in all the clubs that I operate. Having one or two extraordinarily talented individuals can never compare with having a group of untalented, hardworking, system-believing people focused on one common success story. I feel that of all the personal training systems that I have seen in the 35 clubs that I have managed, this system has topped them all!

Soon after this program was developed, there was another large acquisition in California. The two largest health club companies merged and tried to combine their systems, leaving behind some of the secrets that built these wonderful organizations. I have had the privilege to see both systems at work in clubs all over the world. Chicago to Nevada, California to China! The words and systems used in this book will unmistakably without a doubt improve your ability to sell fitness.

Chapter 4

PERSONAL TRAINER PLANNER

Training materials should be kept in the front of your planner and should be referenced as often as possible or whenever needed. As discussed in Chapter 3, I prefer my trainers to memorize various scripts for different situations. Memorizing these various scripts is the first thing a new personal trainer should do. If you are unable to memorize the ten or so pages of script, you should do nothing else until you perfect that area of your arsenal. If you are not able to perform an effective orientation appointment, if you do not know how to present personal training or how to set up a take over (TO), then you should practice in these areas before taking any guests. Once these scripts are memorized, such as the introduction, then these training materials will be used as a reference and training tool. It sounds like a lot of work, but believe me it makes the job easier and more profitable.

Once a month you should train in each area of the book. If you do this, your sales skills will remain sharp and you will have the ability to learn and grow. Remember the fitness industry is a rapidly growing business and change is essential for continued growth and improvement. If certain areas of the training process are not working or you are not improving, then you, as a professional, have to improve the training information you are using.

To-Do List

I found that the personal to-do list is a simple and effective tool that has been used for years by everyone from the common housewife to the President of the United States. It is a simple concept.

When you think of something that is important, write it down! This will put it on your priority list, limiting mistakes and leaving your mind free to think of other things. You can cross off each task as you accomplish it and remaining items can be circled and transferred to the next day's to-do list. This can be an effective habit. I find that people who use this simple tool are more efficient, make fewer mistakes, and get more accomplished. Although this is your business planner, personal matters can still be taken care of at work. It is okay to list personal matters on your to-do list.

Goals and Projections

Goals and projections should be updated daily. This is the most functional way of learning how your production can influence your numbers. As the old saying goes, "the numbers do not lie." This is especially true in our business. The numbers tell us what we are doing right and what we are doing wrong. The numbers are our guides to success. They will show you what happens when you have a bad day, and they will show you what happens when you have a good day. Most importantly, they will show you what happens when you are not set up for that day.

My definition of a successful person is a person that can set goals and then achieve those goals

What happens to your paycheck when you hit your goals? I bet you can answer that question for yourself. Having an organized "Goals and Projections" section in your planner will show you what you have to do daily; it gives you the ability to control your numbers more consistently and will offer you a daily affirmation of your goals. I prefer to track every area of sales separately. Within each area, I have five steps:

Gross Sales: goal, last day worked, month to date, projection and percentage

EFT: goal, last day worked, month to date, projection and percentage

Personal Training: goal, last day worked, month to date, projection and percentage

Supplements: goal, last day worked, month to date, projection andpercentage

Retail: goal, last day worked, month to date, projection and percentage

Other goals: last day worked, month to date, projection and percentage

If kept updated consistently and correctly, these areas will keep us more organized and help increase our sales. We begin by setting goals and then use our materials to project our progress as we go along. Each month you should set goals based on the previous month's performance. Like most successful salespeople, your sales goal should increase each month, as your ability to hit these goals increases. As you hone your sales skills, your comfort level and confidence increase enabling you to achieve higher goals. I personally never set goals that are too easy to achieve. At the same time, I never set goals that are impossible to achieve. You want the goal to be lofty enough to motivate you but not so high that you cannot achieve it. The goal should be in line with what you want your paycheck to be. If you set a goal that is $200,000 in sales and your commission is 10 percent, you will earn $20,000 commission before taxes, therefore, you cannot expect to bring home a $30,000 paycheck! The first goal that should be set is what you want your income to be. Based on that, you can calculate how much you need to sell. You now have your goal.

For Example:

Your desired income is $50,000	50,000
Your commission from each sale is 10%	x10
You must sell	$500,000

Being able to meet your goals will make you a highly effective personal trainer and you will be able to control your financial destiny. The sky is the limit! The last day worked column is what you sold the last day in each area. The month to date column is a running total; it represents the updated total amount you have sold up to that date for the month. The projection column is the month to date divided by the days gone by, times the total days in the month. The percentage column is your projection divided by your goal.

For Example for Projection:

month to date   divided by days gone by.

    x

Total days in the month. = Projection

It is the second day of a 30-day month. Yesterday you sold $2,000 in gross sales. Your month to date is $2,000. One day has gone by, and so you divide 2000 by 1 times 30 days in the month. It means that the total amount you are projecting is $60,000. Divide that by your goal of $70,000. You are at 86 percent of your goal.

For example:

$$\frac{2{,}000 \times 30}{1} = \frac{60{,}000}{70{,}000} = 86\%$$

You now have 29 days left in the month to reach your goal. Since you sold $2,000 on the first day of the month, you now have only $68,000 left to reach your goal. In order to find your daily goal you must minus your month to date, from your goal and divide by how many days are left in the month. The numbers show that you must sell an average of $2,344 per day for the rest of the month to achieve 100 percent of your original goal.

For example:

$$\begin{array}{l} 70{,}000 \\ \underline{- 2{,}000} \\ 68{,}000 \end{array} \qquad \frac{68{,}000}{29} = \mathbf{\$2{,}344}$$

Updating your statistics is something that should be done every day. You should make this a strict habit and it should be the first thing you do every morning after you walk through the club. The numbers, good or bad, will show you the areas that you have to focus on for that day. They also show the areas that you are doing well in and the areas that need improvement.

Finally, your daily appointment sheets will have areas for all important appointment information. Each day's sheet will have sections for logging the time of the appointment, for confirmation, the person's name, their work and home telephone number, a note about the appointment, and finally, the outcome.

Appointments

The **time** section stands for what time you are scheduling the appointment. You write the individual's information next to the time they are expected to arrive for their appointment. You should highlight certain areas of the day to be filled in by the front desk and/or the sales staff to ensure that your appointment book is filled with high quality orientations. The **confirmation** box will allow you to make a note if the appointment has been confirmed. In addition one should check the book regularly to see if any new appointments have been scheduled. It is also advisable to call and reconfirm prior to an appointment to save you from being inconvenienced, for example driving into work only to have to leave again. Finally, ensure that all of your clients are able to contact you at anytime with last minute cancellations. (Please see chapter 28, page 96, Confirming appointments and cancellations.)

Chapter 5

THE LANGUAGE OF SALES

REJECTION WORDS	ACCEPTABLE SUBSTITUTES
Contract	Personal Training Agreement, Agreement, Paperwork, Form
Cost or Price	Investment or Amount
Down Payment	Initial Investment, Initial Amount, One-time Investment
Monthly Payment	Monthly Investment or Monthly Amount
Sell or Sold	Get involved or Get started
Deal	Package or Opportunity
Pay For	Take care of
Sign	Authorize, Approve, Endorse, OK it
Crowded	Popular, Exciting, Active Environment
Salesperson	Fitness Counselor, Trainer, Personal Trainer,
Dollars	Omit this word altogether—the only possible exception is when the guest is comparison shopping, and your club is a better value because it will save him or her so many dollars per month or year

Commission	Fee for service
Objection	Concern
If	When
Cheap	Affordable
Diet	Nutritional Program, Food Intake
Pitch, Spiel.	Presentation
High Pressure	Enthusiasm, Concern
Prizewinner, "up" here	Guest, Client, Member
On a free pass or walk-in	
Sign up, join.	Get involved, Get started

It is important to know that certain words can create an emotional response from your prospective personal training client. It is important to practice and use only the words that are going to work in your favor.

For Example

"Mom I'm going to the health club to get a membership." The mother responds, "Make sure you don't sign anything without reading it first and make sure you don't get involved in any contracts!"

People remember these little things. I don't know why but they just seem to pop up when we use certain words. So practice using the right words and your job will be a lot easier, just like second nature.

Chapter 6

HOW TO SPEAK TO A GUEST

Building instant rapport can come from something as simple as addressing a person by their first name.

A true sales professional and personal trainer understands the basic fundamentals when it comes to speaking to a potential client. Rapport and comfort levels with a client can be created or destroyed almost immediately.

It may sound redundant, but make certain to do the following:

1. Smile, use a firm handshake and maintain eye contact.

2. A proper greeting and introduction is essential. Be sure to introduce yourself and use the client's name.

3. Build rapport by asking many questions. A proper needs analysis can be the key to making the sale. Do not give up too much information before you truly understand your potential client's intentions. (Use your clubs orientation card and perform a proper needs analysis.)

4. Be kind and courteous at all times and be sure to let your client do most of the talking. (**You have two ears and one mouth for a reason!**)

5. It is important to remain indirect when attempting to close the sale. You must develop the ability to maintain good rapport through five closing attempts. (This will only happen if you use the steps outlined in Chapter 16, How to Overcome Objections.)

Sales language

Only seven percent of all communication is verbal which is a fact that many people find hard to believe. Ninety-three percent of our communication has nothing to do with the words that you produce, but more so to do with the non-verbal communication that we use. Non-verbal communication consists of tone of voice, eye contact, facial expressions, and proximity to another person. All of these factors come into play when you're communicating with another individual. A sales person or personal trainer's inability to endear this concept can very easily limit their revenue production and personal income levels. Let's look at this scenario:

One trainer presents a personal training package to a prospective client, but they do not purchase it. Another trainer steps in and performs a full transference of emotions into that prospective client and sells them a package while using the exact same words that the first trainer used. The reason why this happens is that you may be talking to your client, but you are not really *communicating* with them. A full transference of emotions is making your prospect feel what you are feeling, the passion for fitness and the need for proper education through a personal trainer!

There are different ways to communicate the same words, each providing a different meaning to the receiver. You can look at someone and smile, then laugh and call him or her a name. You can also scream in someone's face and call him or her a name. These are two vastly different forms of communication with totally different meanings. They will also achieve two totally different results. You have to be aware of how and what you are communicating. You must help your prospect to understand that you truly care and want to help them attain their personal goals. These are techniques that come naturally to some people and are often difficult to teach. It takes a lot of trial and error. Some people pick up the knack of communicating, or they may have learned naturally through their parents. The bottom-line is that it is very important to pin point the communication style of your guest.

The true meaning of sales is the transference of emotions. Your prospect needs to truly feel and believe in what you are saying. You will come to the point where you learn how to manipulate through communication. This happens once you have memorized the scripts, inserted your personality into them, and effectively learned how to "mirror" your prospect. These certain forms of communication are less verbal than you may think. The first step in learning the sales process is verbal communication: saying the right words, asking the right questions, getting the person to agree by "using tie downs,"all the things that can come across the desk verbally. The T.O. process will enable you to watch your manager and listen to other salespeople who may be better than or more experienced than you. You will begin to learn that there are other areas of communication such as the non-verbal. This form of communication creates the certain energy that flows across the desk and can't be heard. Have you ever shown a guest the prices and observed their face turning red? No doubt you start to sense the friction at the table even tough they haven't said a word. You can clearly see the non-verbal communication coming across the table, the red face and the moving in the seat. You can feel all of the emotions that your guest is projecting. That flow of energy coming across the desk is what I am talking about. A professional knows how to harness and control that energy and use it to close more packages.

Why do you get up from a sales presentation? What does it accomplish? Why do we do that? It clears the air of all the emotions that were flowing back and forth between you and the guest, and enables them to relax. One of your goals is to comfort your client, which can be achieved by helping them to loosen up and feel good about making a purchase. They can't do that if they feel the friction across the desk. There is no denying that people project energy and you should make sure that you are aware of this. Study this and know that it can hold you back from making sales.

You can say all the right things to a guest and everything may seem to be going good, but there is still something missing. What is it? They feel uncomfortable and uneasy about buying a package from you. You said all the right things and were nice to the person, but deep down inside the potential client felt that you weren't being honest or they felt that something just wasn't right. The greeting and introduction is an overlooked but vital aspect of our business. Many sales managers and fitness consultants neglect to devise a uniform greeting strategy when faced with a prospective member.

Greeting and Introduction

This is an area that, when focused on correctly, will improve the relationship with the client, decrease tension and ultimately lead to an increase of sales. There are many different ways of doing this but remember that, "you never get a second chance to make a first impression." See the following script as an example of the method that I prefer to use in this situation.

"How are you?" (Wait for response)

"My name is John, and what is your name?" (Wait for response)

"Mr. Soon to be client, what I would like to do is take a moment of your time to find out exactly what you are looking to accomplish? Then I will ask you a couple of questions in regard to your current fitness level and goals in the facility. Finally when we are finished, I will take you through some basic exercises. Sound fair?" (Wait for response)

"Great."

Since I believe in a consistent system approach, I feel it is important to avoid making the introduction too complicated. Many trainers will not use a system approach for fear it will limit their personality and many employers fear that they may not be able to successfully teach it to new employees. They view it as more of a burden than it is worth, avoiding the implementation of a standard introduction and presentation, which can, in effect, be detrimental to sales.

Building Rapport

In order to consistently produce sales of any type, one must build rapport with a prospective client. Building good rapport allows you to build a comfort zone and a trust between yourself and the prospect. If there is no trust, there is no sale.

You must attempt to think as they would think and you must be patient and mindful of their questions and concerns. People rarely trust those they do not like or feel comfortable with. Being humble and kind in all situations will help to earn this trust.

Take a moment to think of the people you surround yourself with. I am going to guess that you probably trust and like the people that you call "friends". The most successful sales people in this business build mini-relationships with the majority of their prospects. Having good rapport means that you communicate well with another person, you are friendly, and you trust one another. If you think of each prospect as a potential friend, you will immediately find yourself more comfortable when speaking with them. The easiest way to build a strong rapport with your prospect is by uncovering possible common interests that you may have. It is easy for a person to say "no" to a person they do not like, or a person they have nothing in common with. Remember the **K-I-S-S** rule. It means **K**eep **I**t **S**imple **S**tupid! Even though you want to build rapport and find common interests, you want to do this in a simple, comfortable fashion. Be careful not to offer too much information about yourself before discovering what their interests are. Ask your prospect questions and find common interests based on their answers. Giving up too much information about yourself before you know the interests of your client can cause problems that are hard to overcome.

For example, John is attempting to sell a personal training package to Tom. Tom explains that he is a huge football fan, he lives in the Bay Area, and football is his life. John replies that the Bay Area is a beautiful place, and he loves San Francisco. "Go 49ers!" Tom explains that he lives in Oakland, and he is a Raiders fan!

In this situation, the salesperson did not find out the proper information before speaking. The salesperson was too quick with his response and did not pre-qualify. Therefore, since Tom's life is football, now opposite interests have been established and John's sale is now increasingly more difficult. The salesperson/prospect relationship is one of give and take. You will find yourself in situations where you share no common interests with a prospect. In fact, you are not going to care in the least about some of their interests and quite often you will find yourself disagreeing with their opinions. These are the times when you must remember that you are a professional, not a fan, and you are the one who must stay in control. Always try to keep a smile on your face and keep after *your* goal.

Mirroring and Matching

Along with memorizing your scripts, you must learn to "mirror" your prospects. "Mirroring" allows one to build rapport by utilizing the same voice tones, facial expressions, and body language as the person they are engaging. We will always feel more comfortable with someone that we feel parity with. The most successful sales people in the world not only find common bonds verbally, but do so physically as well. This is a very vital and overlooked aspect of being a personal trainer and a salesperson. You **must** find common ground with your potential client as this can be the difference between gaining a new client and losing one. When used properly, mirroring means to have the ability to change the way you act, talk, and the speed in which you react or walk in accordance with the prospective client. This is not something that I can outline for you. It is not something that is easy to teach. It is an effective tool that, when mastered, can make an unbelievable impact on your sales numbers and your income.

For Example:

If the prospect is shy, you cannot be aggressive. If you have a prospect that walks slowly, you cannot walk fast. If your prospect talks quietly, you need to talk quietly. If your prospect leans back and crosses their legs during your sales presentation, you need to do so as well. Get the picture?

This area of your arsenal can go much deeper. You have to be like a chameleon, a lizard that has the ability to change its color and shape to meet its surroundings.

Chapter 7

THE FITNESS ORIENTATION

The fitness orientation or complimentary workout has become a very important aspect of the personal training sales process. As the personal training sales process began to evolve, we found that the most difficult obstacle to overcome was getting the personal trainers to go out on the floor and take a member through a complimentary workout. It has proven to be difficult to get trainers to approach members and offer their services. We felt that the key to a successful health club operation must lie in getting our members results. We found that most of the members that dropped out of the club were the ones that didn't see any results within the first 6 weeks. As a remedy to these two problems, we developed a program that would benefit trainers and members alike. It would give the trainers an opportunity to offer their services as well as giving every single member an opportunity to work with a trainer possessing the knowledge to set a successful program in motion. This program could show the benefits and the value of the one-on-one personal training program. We truly felt that the success of the personal training department and the health club would depend on producing quality opportunities for the trainers. We also felt that every individual who joined the club should get a chance to experience some fitness education. At that time, we made the decision that every person, whether they joined on a membership or were given a free pass to the club, would receive three sessions with a personal trainer. At the end of the third session, they would be brought to the table and given a presentation or talk about how their orientation went. We would also find out what vitamins they needed and if they were interested in continuing with one-on-one personal training.

Keep Them Coming

In order to be a successful trainer you must keep a consistent influx of new clients coming your way. There are several ways of doing this. One way is to be able to work the floor. The other way is to produce a great line of quality buddy referrals. The only problem with this is that they require a natural sales ability. We have found that many trainers were unable to use this system consistently. The best trainers in our business were the ones that had the ability to pick and choose clients based on consistent re-signing of clients, continued orientation sign ups, and a dedication toward reaching their goals. If you maintain a consistent approach towards creating daily orientations you will be booked with quality personal training clients. The over sold clients can easily be passed down to other trainers in the club that have fewer clients or may just be starting out. Pick and choose the clients you work well with. Build a relationship with other personal trainers, and allocate a system to send over bookings to these newer or less fortunate team members. Remember the more quality clients you train and maintain, the more you can charge for your service.

In review, every member who joined the club was offered three free forty minute training sessions to orientate the members to the club. The original program consisted of a three step process the first #1 a questionnaire and a fitness assessment followed by a short test. The second #2 session consisted of a brief cardio introduction and a split 50% body resistance workout. The third #3 session consisted of the unused muscle from the previous day and a brief presentation of the benefits of other club services and one-on-one personal training.

The Orientation Card

I felt that the early orientation program worked well and produced great numbers. The program that I now recommend for best results has come from a modified system that has been tested, tried and improved. Your orientation cards or questionnaires will vary from club to club depending on your particular demographic. It is important to understand that your particular company has put a lot of time and effort into creating this service to the members. I believe that if you have been properly trained and you do a quality orientation, you will find that in most cases your club has created substantial value using their orientation card. Looking at the orientation program from an ownership stand point, most companies have determined that this program has substantial cost involved and many of the large health clubs chains have shortened this program to meet financial obligations. Whether your company offers one complimentary session or ongoing sessions, the fact remains the same. Offering free personal training and using your company's standardized goal sheet will improve your selling ability.

Here are some pointers:

- Scheduling quality orientations and making sure that you have several each and everyday will improve your business.

- Book orientations for times that you have openings in your schedule. Most likely your potential clients will book their orientation at the same time they are interested in receiving the one-on-one personal training sessions

- It is important to use the communication skills outlined in Chapter 6 and to build rapport with your potential client. Even if the member is not interested in ongoing sessions, they are still very important to the club and your first impression may be a lasting one.

- It is important to be informative but equally important to ask questions, make notes and pay close attention to the education level of your potential client. Using technical information may overwhelm or invoke fear.

- It is important to spend some time on the written part of the interview but it is also equally important to spend time building rapport and not focusing so much on the technical and the written parts of the interview. Spending more time understanding the person can be more important than the fitness.

• Normally, as a rule of thumb, we do not present personal training on the first orientation. In some cases, your potential client may show an interest in one-on-one sessions during your first interview. If this were the case, I would recommend doing a full presentation on the one-on-one sessions available.

• Depending on which presentation you like best, I would recommend learning it word for word until you are so comfortable that you can add your own personality and style. Once you have done this, your presentation should sound smooth and should not sound memorized.

Chapter 8

THE QUICK RESULTS WORKOUT CARD

Date:_____   FA1   FA2

Guest Name:_____   _____ _____

Trainer:_____

Name:_____ Date of birth:_____Age:_____

Address: _____

Phone:(H)_____(O)_____(HP)_____

E-mail:_____ Occupation:_____

Emergency Contact:_____

<u>Health Screening</u>
Have you had or every experienced:

- ❑ Dizziness or fainting?
- ❑ Any heart condition
- ❑ High(low)Blood pressure
- ❑ Stroke
- ❑ Diabetes

- ❑ Any pain or injury to the joints
- ❑ Pregnant or given birth in the past 1 year
- ❑ Any major surgery
- ❑ Any other medical conditions that we
- ❑ should be aware of?

I am aware that physical exercise can subject me to serious injury and that if I engage in physical activity or use any Number One Fitness facility or participate in any Number One Fitness sponsored event I do so entirely at my own risk. I release Number One Fitness and its directors, officers, and agents from any liability to me or damage or loss to any of my personal property in connection with my use of Number One Fitness facilities or equipment or my participation in Number One Fitness sponsored activities. I understand that I am giving up legal rights that I might otherwise have and that this release includes without limitation, damages I may suffer as a result of (1) my use of any exercise equipment, product or Number One Fitness facility, (ii) the malfunctioning of any Number One Fitness equipment, (iii) any Number One Fitness instruction or supervision, and (iv) slipping, falling, or otherwise injuring myself in any manner while on the Number One Fitness premises, including sidewalks and parking.

Member Signaure:_____Date:_____

Fitness Goals

Please check on the goals you want to achieve in embarking on an exercise program:

❑ Improve cardiovascular fitness   ❑ Improve flexibility

❑ Improve on a sport specific performance   ❑ Reduce body fat

❑ Sculpting and toning   ❑ Increasing energy level

❑ Increase muscle mass   ❑ Ability to cope with stress

❑ Increase strength   ❑ Social

On the scale of 1-5, how would you rate your current fitness level? (1, 2, 3, 4, 5)

Can you give a brief description of your current fitness activity for one week?

_____

When was the last time that you felt that your fitness level met or exceeded acceptable levels?

_____

Please list a brief description of an average nutrient intake over a two day period. Please include alcohol, coffee, cigarette, prescription or dietary drugs.

_____

What is the most convenient time for exercise, morning, afternoon or evening?

_____

What is your current work or school schedule?

_____

How much time would you be allocating towards accomplishing your fitness goals? _____

	Date:	Date:		Before	After
Weight	lbs	lbs	Neck		
Blood Pressure	Mm Hg	Mm Hg	Shoulder		
			Elbow		
RHR	bpm	bpm	Wrist		
Fat composition / weight	%	%	Waist		
			Hip		
	lbs	lbs	Knee		
			Ankle		
Lean tissue comp. / wt.	%	%			
	lbs	lbs			
H2O	%	%			
	lbs	lbs			
BMI	Kg/m2	Kg/m2			
chest	inch	inch			
waist	inch	inch			
hips	inch	inch			
thigh	inch	inch			
arm	inch	inch			

Chapter 9

INTRODUCTION TO THE PRE-SCRIPTIVE PRESENTATION

After you have taken your member or guest through a fitness orientation they should have some understanding of the benefits of the program. Make sure that you are sitting down and then take a moment to review the orientation card. This way you may refer to and clarify any of the notes that you had taken out on the floor. After finishing a brief outline of the results it is time for you to use your six-step presentation. **This is a very pivotal moment and your success depends upon your diligence in reference to preparation. Do you know the presentation word for word? The difference between success and failure will, in most cases come from ones ability to prepare.** The first part of the presentation should be the benefits building process. The script that I recommend will follow the steps that I have outlined in chapter 10 and will add value to your presentation. The following is a script that was developed by the same personal trainer and regional supervisor at one of the pioneering personal training clubs in California. The revenue and service produced by his personal training teams still stand up to any modern day challenges. This script has been modified by thousands of health clubs world-wide who have used it to produce and generate income from their personal training departments. Although, I do not endorse or use this script in my clubs, it definitely works. As a person in a management position and as a part of a team, I have always felt that it is important to follow a company system. I have worked in many clubs that have used this personal training presentation with great success. Whenever I found myself in a position where a company used or endorsed this presentation I used it as my only form of sell-ing technique. Again, it is important to have a presentation that helps the guest to realize what they are paying their hard earned money for. Therefore, you have to paint a picture in a person's mind of the benefits they will be receiving from your service. If the benefits out-weigh the monetary loss your member or guest will be willing the make the trade, money for results.

Closing the Sale

Your prospective client will give you the same objections that you will likely hear when you are trying to sell a membership. You will hear everything from "I want to try it out on my own", to "I want to think about it", or "I need to speak to my spouse." It is important to understand that as we are selling anything, especially sales in a health club, your "be back" sales ratio will be very low. Studies have shown that 60% of customers will say no five times before they will say yes, thus it is important to try to overcome the objections when closing a personal training presentation. If you are a new personal trainer, I would imagine that the most difficult task facing you would be getting and keeping quality clients. You should allocate a percent-age of your time every day towards becoming the ultimate in your trade and you must remember to focus on all aspects of being a pro-fessional. It is not okay to disregard one area of your arsenal. This is a book on how to sell personal training. It does focus mainly on sell-ing and retaining a quality stream of income, but it is also a large part of the bigger picture and should ultimately improve your overall suc-cess.

Chapter 10

THE SIX STEPS TO A

PROFESSIONALLY STRUCTURED

FITNESS PROGRAM

Mr. soon to be client 50-60% of your success in the club can come from **Food Intake**. In order to see optimum results, your trainer will maintain the proper percentage of proteins, carbohydrates and fats. This will ensure satiation. For example: if your goal is weight loss, what your trainer is going to do is work with foods that are convenient for your life style. Based on that information your trainer will customize a caloric deficit. This deficit may consist of a thousand calories a day.

Proper Cardiovascular exercise is the stimulus necessary to mobilize fat or excess calories for fuel. Adding additional cardiovascular exercise will cause your body to burn more energy. Your trainer will customize a cardiovascular exercise program within the proper heart rate zones. This stimulus will create an additional thousand calorie deficit.

As you can see in the first two steps; through proper food intake and proper cardiovascular exercise, we have eliminated two thousand calories from your body. The laws of thermo-dynamics demand that your body begin to reduce in size and weight. But we have also created the biggest enemy in regards to weight loss. HUNGER. To replace the deficit your body needs nutrients. But most of the time the body fills that nutrient gap with food. The problem with that is by adding food you also add calories. Therefore change becomes difficult. We will replace the lost nutrients with **Supplementation,** thus creating the prefect environment for change.

Resistance Training. Your Trainer will design and customize a workout program specifically for you, muscle equals metabolism. The more quality lean muscle you have, the more your body will continue to burn fat 24 hours a day. I am sure if you are like everyone else you would love to burn fat while you are sleeping.

Two vital but overlooked areas of your fitness success will come from **Rest and Flexibility**. During an intense workout session, each and every cell in your body will go through a period of transformation; without the proper replenishment and rest your body will be unable to benefit from the exercise. Not only is flexibility essential in the prevention of injury but it also ensures that your body maintains its proper elasticity. This will ensure full range of motion, rapid recovery, and full muscle development. Do you see the effects of rest and flexibility?

Professional Assistance along with food intake this may be the most essential part of your fitness success. Your professional trainer will ensure success by manipulating the above five variables so that your body does not level off in regard to the exercise programs. Your trainer will then change and adapt so that you may avoid plateaus and continue to see changes towards accomplishing all of your fitness goals in and out of the club.

Chapter 11

PRICE PRESENTATION

The Price Presentation

The price presentation that is used for prescriptive personal training selling is based on the personal trainer being similar to a doctor. The personal trainer will lay out details about your goal. Then based on your goal, the personal trainer will give you precise information on both the time, and amount of personal training sessions that are required in order to effectively accomplish your goal. Once the trainer has determined the amount of weight loss or muscle gain that the potential client may be interested in achieving, the trainer will then prescribe the number of times per week and the total number of weeks that the client must meet with the trainer. For example, the trainer may say "Mr. Johnson you said that your goal was to lose ten pounds?" Mr. Johnson says, "That's right." "Well, based on our laws of thermo-dynamics, we found that the average person interested in losing weight must meet three times a week with a personal trainer." "The average healthy limit for weight loss is about a pound and a half a week." "Based on my professional opinion as your personal training and weight loss specialist, I recommend that you enroll in a three time a week personal training program with a certified professional." "Also based on our law of thermo-dynamics you should be able to lose the weight in seven weeks." "Does this make sense to you?" "Yes!" At that point, the trainer will ask; cash, check or credit card. The member usually appears to be somewhat shocked. As the personal trainer begins to complete the paper work, the member or guest may try to back out of the financial part of the agreement. Many times, just being assumptive will help create a smooth transition towards completing the sale. This is not my favorite or preferred way to present prices but it is definitely effective. I have spent many years in the health club business and I have witnessed many things that work and are successful. The goal of my training is not to reinvent nor is it to pick and choose scripts that I think are the best. This personal training presentation works. It is up to you to decide which presentation best suits your personality and style.

EXAMPLE: x marks the spot for the days and weeks that the client must meet with the trainer.

PERSONAL TRAINING GOAL SHEET   NO# 1

GOAL_____100% OF YOUR GOAL WEEKS____ DAYS___

	Monday	Tuesday	Wednesday	Thursday	Friday	Saturday	Sunday
Week 1	X		X		X		
Week 2	X		X		X		
Week 3	X		X		X		
Week 4	X		X		X		
Week 5	X		X		X		
Week 6	X		X		X		
Week 7	X		X		X		
Week 8							
Week 9							
Week 10							
Week 11							
Week 12							
Week 13							
Week 14							

THE HEALTHY ACHIEVABLE LIMIT FOR WEIGHT LOSS IS ABOUT 1 AND A HALF POUNDS A WEEK.

THE HEALTHY ACHIEVABLE LIMIT FOR MUSCLE GAIN IS ABOUT 1 POUND A WEEK.

1 session 70 10 sessions 60 20 sessions 50 40 sessions 40

Chapter 12

MY PERSONAL TRAINING PRESENTATION

This is the point where I am given the opportunity to reveal the presentation that really changed the face of fitness. For the majority of the trainers back in the days when these pilot programs were being developed, selling their service was the last thing on their mind. The personal trainer was just a guy or girl out on the floor that helped give some good pointers and maybe once in awhile, if you were lucky or good looking, you would get some rich old person to pay money to have you teach them how to workout. Most of the trainers honestly believed that the service they provided was reserved only for a certain class! If I was to "stereo-type;" the average young, new fitness trainer did not believe in their own self worth and to most young trainers 50 dollars for 1 hour of their training services was just an unheard of amount of money. So, we decided to make it our goal to find out where the shortcomings were in the personal training area. Once we pinpointed what the shortcomings actually were, we set our goal and then we developed a plan of how we would overcome each of our obstacles. It may sound rather scientific but this was a business plan and we confronted it accordingly. We realized that the Personal Training department could be one of the fastest growing revenue centers in our clubs. We believed that we could set ourselves apart by offering the most successful program to our members. We truly believed that we could create a way of life that generated results. If we could teach our members that by using private training sessions to develop good effective habits people from all walks of life would be able to enjoy the benefits of personal training. A large percentage of top athletes, successful movie actors, and even executives have worked with professional trainers to achieve maximum results. We knew what the major key to our business was, always stay focused and remember that the main obstacle would be getting results. It was also important that we understand a successful system for learning how to sell personal training. We believed that the first step in selling personal training was to get potential clients in front of a trainer so that they would understand what it is that the trainers do. The second step is that you must understand the benefits of the one-on-one program. The third step is to develop a presentation that builds the value of this extremely precious program. The fourth step is presenting the different price options and the fifth step is getting the commitment and closing the sale.

Step One: Understanding What It Is the Trainers Do

We believed that the trainers needed a benefits building program that would be so powerful that no closing was necessary, the following is what was created. The trainers do *goal setting* for the member, setting achievable goals within a specific time frame and putting everything down on paper. This ensures that the member can track their improvement. The trainers also focus on other important areas such as those outlined below.

Food intake, working with the type of food that members like to eat.

Accountability, ensuring that the members show up to their scheduled appointments.

Consistency, making sure that the member is working out on a consistent basis, about 3 to 4 times per week.

Motivation, is needed to consistently hit your goals and ensure that you get the most out of every single workout.

Proper Techniques to avoid injuries and to ensure the optimal benefit to the member.

Program Design, individualizing the program to achieve long-term results and a lifetime education of fitness. Tie downs were added at the end of each step to gain minor agreement.

Step Two: The Benefits of Personal Training

The benefits of personal training are endless, but I will single out a few: a better, longer life through exercise; an education that will stay with you for the duration of your life; better self-esteem; a positive impact on your personal relationships; better performance at work; more energy; healthy meal planning; and lower stress levels. This is just a portion of the benefits. The possibilities are endless.

Step Three: The Presentation of Benefits

I personally recommend that you come up with a script that will build up the benefits and add value to your presentation. I used a script developed by one of the top personal trainers in our company at the time. Your script may resemble a script like this one (refer to chapter 13, page 33) or the one I recommended previously for the greeting and introduction. I worked with an outstanding trainer who lent his script to all the salespeople to help them increase personal training sales. It was three pages long and it took me a month to memorize, but it worked great. The first month I used the presentation my sales went through the roof and I sold $9,000 in personal training. It focuses on building the benefits of the training program and helps the guest to understand exactly what they are paying $50 an hour for. Remember, you cannot show a person in one hour precisely what it is the personal trainer is going to help them accomplish. Therefore, you have to paint a picture in the persons' mind of the benefits they are going to receive from this service. If the benefits outweigh the loss, your member will be willing to make the trade, money for results.

Step Four: Price Presentation

You should have a price presentation that has several different options and programs. There should be a program to fit every budget from executives to students. The program should be able to meet the needs of all the individual goals. There are many different goals that the members will have. A few of the most common are weight loss, weight gain, rehabilitation, toning and firming programs, and a basic introduction to fitness. Your club should have packages priced from $50 to $5,000 and sessions that range from one to fifty. These are the standard pricing ranges and sessions that most successful clubs have. The presentations at your particular club will vary so you should check with your fellow trainers to ensure consistency.

Step Five: Closing the Sale

Your perspective client will give you the exact same objections that you will get when you are trying to sell anything. You will hear everything from "I need to think about it" to "I need to talk it over with my husband". Your closing techniques should be the same as with a membership and you should include everything from "TO'ing" to "price dropping" to "post dated checks". You will even use commitment questions such as "If I could get you a good deal would you want to commit to achieving your personal training goals today?" You have to realize that personal training accounts for approximately 30% of the gross sales in fitness centers today. Your members in the gym are willing to spend their money and time because they are interested in achieving long-term results. Personal training is the most effective method the members can rely on in order to achieve those results. This is a very important aspect of what we do and if you cannot master this area, you will never be a complete professional, and you will be left behind in our industry.

Chapter 13

MY PERSONAL TRAINING SCRIPT

Memorize, Utilize, Maximize Your Success

Mr. Prospect, the starting point of personal training is goal setting. It's about setting a target of what you want to achieve because if you can't see your target, how are you going to hit it? Right?

Have you ever set goals before? What your trainer is going to do is set challenging, believable, achievable goals within a specific time frame, then put them down on paper so now they become measurable.

Proper food intake also plays a big role. About 60 to 70 percent of your success in the club is going to be from the things you eat outside the club. How is your diet right now? How many times per day are you eating? What your trainer is going to do is have you bring in two to three days of your current food intake. Do you think that might be something you're able to do?

The third aspect of ensuring your results is the accountability factor. What that means to you is that you will be much more likely to come down to the facility and have a quality workout when you have an appointment set with a certified professional. If for any reason you don't make it in your trainer will be calling you saying, "We can't accomplish your goals if you're not here!" Can you see how that will benefit you?

And accountability over time works out to be consistency. We know that in anything, if we are not consistent, we are not going to be successful. So your trainer ensures that you adhere to your regular exercise program in order to accomplish your goals. We recommend that you meet with your trainer two to three days per week for optimal results. How many days will you be able to commit to working with your trainer?

Now, motivation ties into this because your trainer instills in you a greater degree of commitment to accomplishing your goals. Motivation is the difference between accelerated results and just kind of moving along at a slow rate and I'm sure you're like everyone else and you prefer results sooner rather than later, right?

Proper technique also plays a big role. First to avoid injury, and second, if you aren't doing things correctly you will not be able to get the optimal benefits either from the equipment or for your time.

Now, the "personal" in personal training comes in with program design. This involves your trainer designing a customized program for you and monitoring how your body responds so you maximize every rep, set, and minute in the facility to achieve your goals.

Price Prezo

Now, Mr. Prospect, normally a session of personal training is going to run you $70 per session, but what the company has done to make them more affordable for you as a member is they have grouped them into packages to suit your specific needs. As you can clearly see, the more you show that you are committed to achieving your fitness goals, the lower the rate per session. The first option is great; it's what I call the starter package. It gives you some time to gain knowledge, learn techniques and how to apply them in the club so that you can continue to work toward being successful.

Now, Mr. Prospect, I'm going to skip to this package for now and move on to what I call our accelerated results package. As you can see, when you enroll in a 32-session package with a trainer the rate drops all the way down to $49 per session. The great thing is that this is the one that our most successful members are a part of. This package will put you in the optimal position to achieve your fitness goals through a longer-term commitment and you take advantage of the lowest rate. So you can see that this package is obviously the best value, right? You will really see substantial changes in your body with this package.

Now, I skipped the 16-session package for a very simple reason, Mr. Prospect. This is the most popular package when people enroll in the program on a first-time basis. It's the one that most people in your position go with. It's great because you get a considerably reduced rate and a substantial period of time to work with the trainer and experience the true benefits of the program. During this time you will observe positive results and continued progress.

Now, I will back you in any decision that you make today toward accomplishing your goals. Out of the different options, which one would you be leaning towards?

PERSONAL TRAINING
SINGLE SESSION RATE $70

STARTER PACKAGE **MOST POPULAR** **ACCELERATED RESULTS**

6 SESSIONS **16 SESSIONS** **32 SESSIONS**

60 PER SESSION **55 PER SESSION** **49 PER SESSION**

GOAL SETTING
PROPER FOOD INTAKE
ACCOUNTABILITY
CONSISTENCY
MOTIVATION
PROPER TECHNIQUE
PROGRAM DESIGN

#1 fitness

Chapter 14

HOW AND WHEN TO *T.O.*

T.O. (take over) plays a very important role in the sales learning process. Many sales managers and personal training supervisors will use this technique in the mentoring process. Many of the important and vital communication skills that are developed can only be fully understood at the table. Most of these skills are non-verbal and over time you will develop, improve and have the ability to understand all of the non-verbal codes. This will not happen in a day, but in time you may look at someone's face and recognize when they are scared, not comfortable, or in a hurry. Only experience at the table will give you the instincts to tell right away if the potential client is not interested or in a hurry. Likewise you should be able to tell if your guest just wants to come in and join and be capable of adjusting your techniques adequately. This is what the TOing process is going to teach you. TOing is going to teach you what to say, when to say it and how to react in every situation. Usually when I am training new staff on how to sell, I will make them get up at least five times from the table during each sales presentation. I do this to advise the trainer of the things to say and do during each step of the selling process. This coaching process enables the personal trainer to fully understand all of the variables involved in being the ultimate professional.

Examples: To excuse yourself from the table.

"I will be right back." "Let me get the price sheet/business card for you." "If you give me one moment I can find out the answer for you." "Will you please hold on for a moment?" "Let me go and get a pen / calculator."

The guest is not going to leave. The reason I ask new salespeople or trainers to do this is because I want to be involved as a manager in the selling process. I want them to inform me as to what is happening at the table. Some personal trainers go through the whole sales presentation and don't realize that the guest has their spouse waiting for them, or that there has been a price change. Getting up clears the air and gives you the time and space to get advice, it also enables you regroup or think. It is somewhat similar to a timeout used in sports when things are not going well or to gain momentum. You can only learn so much from listening to yourself talk and you should use other strong closers and trainers to add their strong points to your arsenal.

What is lost when you don't TO? You have lost a chance to learn. You have lost a chance to make more money. You have lost a chance to close a sale. All these things are lost when you do not TO. When I was a new salesperson, I asked the other staff and managers to TO for me all of the time. This step was instrumental in my early selling success.

The most important rule of the T.O.

You *cannot talk!* You cannot say anything. Listen, watch, learn, and feel the energy. The only time you should talk is when your potential client tells a lie to the person who is TOing for you, but this is rare. Ensure that your guest is sitting down as you will rarely sell a personal training package if your potential client is standing up. It is imperative to practice and prepare in regard to getting a guest to sit down, this will strengthen your closing abilities. Here are some basic rules when TOing.

Rule 1: It is better to TO too early than too late. Do not wait until the guest is leaving, standing up, or totally upset before you TO.

Rule 2: If you are a new personal trainer, I recommend that you TO before you give the price. That way your fitness supervisor will be able to gain the commitment from the guest before showing the price.

Rule 3: TO to your manager, fitness supervisor or top producing trainer. Theses are the people you stand to learn the most from.

Rule 4: Do not be afraid to get up. If your guest gives you an objection that you cannot overcome, get up and regroup. (*"Hold on just a second, I will be right back."*)

Rule 5: Make sure the person TOing for you stays until the completion of the sale. The person may feel like the deal was with the person TOing for you, and may bring up new objections once they leave. (Many sales are lost because of this mistake.)

Rule 6: Make sure that your company is on the same page when it comes to giving information. The last thing you would want to happen is for the person doing a TO to give information conflicting with yours.

Rule 7: The most important rule: *You never open your mouth until you know what the shot is*! This refers to making sure the person that is doing the TO is aware of what is going on and does not come in and destroy your sale. A briefing prior to the take over will ensure this does not happen

Rule 8: Last but not least **never ever talk**. Once the TO has begun you have given up your right to talk.

Chapter 15

FILLING OUT THE PERSONAL

TRAINING AGREEMENT

 Most personal trainers tend to lose their sales right when they begin to fill out the paper work or agreement. Most of the time the guest will try to stall by asking questions. They are often hoping to find something in your answer they can use to avoid getting started on the program. Some people find it hard to fully agree to the financial terms. You will see many clients that agree with everything you say but then will then try to find excuses at the end of your presentation in an attempt to find a way out of spending any money or starting the program. Remember, the **K-I-S-S** rule **Keep It Simple Silly**. If you give too much information, the member will find something in your answer that may give them a reason not to get started.

Example: an untrained fitness professional may say, "We are going to get you up early and start your day off with a protein shake, then we will do one hour of cardio and after that we are going to get you going on weight training!" First of all this is not asking a **question** this is making a **statement**. The statement will give the potential client time to "think" of reasons why this won't work. This form of communication lets the clients mind wander! This counterproductive form of communication is the number one mistake made by trainees. In this situation the untrained personal trainer thinks that what they are doing is selling, always try to remember *telling is not selling*.

Always fill out the top of personal training agreement with the personal information yourself. If you give it to the guest, they will stop and hold the pen and start to ask questions. As you fill out the personal information, you want to ask a series of questions that occupy the client's thoughts. If they are answering your questions, their mind is occupied. The thoughts that are going through the mind of the soon to be client are that of **your choosing!** It is now almost impossible for your new client to think of his or her own questions to ask.

For Example:

"It is great that you have decided to join our personal training program, John. John, could you spell your last name? What is your address, and your telephone number? John, did you want to take care of your training program by cash, check, or credit card? And you brought that with you today?" Simply hold up your hand in the shape of a credit card as you continue to write, and they will almost always reach in and grab their purse or wallet. If they do not reach for their form of payment, ask the same question again, *"And you have brought that with you today?"*

It is important to remember that many of the members you will be selling to, may be in their exercise clothes and were not prepared to make a purchase. Most clubs will keep the members credit cards on file or it can be run manually at a later time. At that point, you need to get the client to authorize the training agreement. You do this by simply explaining the agreement while pointing out each area of the agreement with your pen. I always put circles or stars next to the area that needs to be signed. I explain, "John, this is your personal training agreement, we have all of your personal information and you will be getting your copy in a moment. Your total investment today is (whatever the total). Your price per session here as you can see is written clearly. I also wrote the total amount just to guarantee that nothing more is charged to your credit card. To guarantee and lock in the discounted rate, just go ahead and give me your authorization there." If they hesitate, simply tap your finger on the dotted line and say, "right here." If they start to read the agreement, simply tap your finger, and say, "John, I will be giving you a copy, and you can read all the rules and details." Again, remember to keep asking questions until all the signatures are finished. "John, did you want to make your first training appointment today or would tomorrow be better for you?" The membership agreement should be controlled by you the trainer and should never leave your hands. It should be filled out quickly while asking questions. After the guest answers each question, follow immediately with another question.

Overcoming the EFT Objections

Many clubs will offer the members thr use of a charge account and others give the members only one option of paying for the training with cash, check or credit card. Whatever the case may be most clubs will allow the clients to pay for the training in installments. When the clients choose to pay for the package in installments it is important the make sure that payment is "secured." The word secured simply means that we can obtain cash that day if the client doesn't come back! An EFT gives the club authorization to automatically deduct the amount for the member's personal training from either their checking or credit card account. This helps the member by automatically making their payment and keeping their personal training active without the concern of making their payment on time. It benefits the club by having secured access to a check or credit card. This secured billing method is done electronically and uses little time or labor, which will save the club a substantial amount of money in the long run. It also shows the company's stability to potential investors and/or buyers. When I was new in this business I was so afraid of this kind of payment that the potential clients could sense my fear of EFTs. Remember, a large percentage of communication is non-verbal. If you are afraid of EFTs, your guest will sense it and will not be willing to use this method of payment. Many people have had bad experiences with electronic fund transfers in the past, perhaps you are one of them. Using this system, there is rarely a mistake. I will give you several examples of how to present the easy, no hassle monthly personal training program.

Example 1:

"Mary, your personal training is taken care of monthly, and your bank will send our bank a check automatically each month, sound fair?"

Example 2:

"Mary, I know you have had problems in the past with automatic withdrawal, but wouldn't you rather save your money and earn interest on it rather than paying your personal training package in full? The new EFT system at our club is far more advanced than the old systems. It is the safest and the easiest way for you to take care of your training program. I can assure you that if in the unlikely circumstance you were to have any problems you can call me directly, and I will fix it for you immediately. Mary, did you want to pre-pay your package or do our no-hassle plan?"

Example 3:

"Mary, if you do not mind me asking you a question, what would be the difference between the two payment types? You having an EFT monthly for your training or coming into the club to pay are the same thing. The only difference is we do not have the ability to hire a large staff to take all of the client's checks every month. The only difference for you would be if you did not want to pay for your training, and you always take care of your bills, right Mary?"

Example 4:

Mary says, "I do not want anyone to have access to my account." I respond, "Mary, the only one who has access to your account is your bank, and you are authorizing your bank to send our bank $150 per month. We have no access to your bank. Any mistake that would be made would be made by your bank and would be your bank's responsibility. Take a look at the agreement, Mary. It shows that you are authorizing only $150 dollars a month on the first of each month and nothing more."

Example 5:

Mary says, "I do not do anything automatically out of my account." I respond, "Mary, I do not do anything automatically out of my account either. But I think you would agree with me that the fees for my checking account are taken out automatically by my bank. Fees for bounced checks or overdraft charges, new check charges, or annual fees are taken out automatically. So I think we can both agree that the future is going to only leave room for this form of payment. Most companies are even deducting taxes automatically from our directly deposited paychecks. So I think you would agree that in most cases, this is our only option."

Remember that an EFT training program is more convenient for the client, the club, and you. What you as the professional must communicate to the client is that this form of payment exists for their convenience. Like anything else, if they see how the program benefits them and they trust what you say, they will be more likely to agree to it.

Chapter 16

HOW TO OVERCOME OBJECTIONS

The seven most common objections you will hear will be the weaponry used by the members to stop you from getting them results. These procrastination techniques have been used successfully for years and will prevent you from selling packages. The sooner you learn how to overcome them, the sooner you will be able to start to help people to improve their lives. Getting your clients enrolled in a personal training package will be almost impossible if you don't learn to overcome the following seven common obstacles.

- Spouse /parent (I want to talk to my husband or wife. Mom or dad.)
- My friend is going to train me.
- Time (I don't have it.)
- Try it out (I want to try it on my own.)
- Think about it (I will be back.)
- Group/Friends (I have a friend and we want to workout together.)
- Too expensive

How long will you wait to learn how to overcome this weaponry? Clients will use the above, as well as other objections against you on a daily basis. The sooner you feel comfortable hearing the excuses and overcoming them, the sooner you can improve as a personal trainer. DRILL! DRILL! DRILL!

How to Handle Objections:

1. Hear them out. If you cannot hear the problem, you will not be able to understand their concerns.

2. Feed it back to them in question form, "You want to think about it"?

3. Show empathy. "You want to think about it? I can understand you want to think about it. This is a big decision. "Other serious people just like you, have felt the same way."

Remember Three Key Words:

Feel: "I can understand the way you feel."

Felt: "Other people have felt the same way."

Found: "But what we have found is that once you have started your training program, it will be the best decision you have ever made."

4. Isolate: "Other than thinking about it, is there anything else preventing you from enrolling in this package today?"

5. Overcome: "What if it was only $10 Per session, would you still want to think about it?" **"No?"** "So it is mainly the money."

6. Get it down to money. We cannot control what their husband is going to say, whether or not they want to try it on their own, or whether or not they have the time. But we can change the price. We can work with different package options to fit their individual needs.

Although it is important to use the steps outlined in this chapter, it is also important to know that there are other ways to close a sale. The first closing technique that I teach my trainers is a very simple one. It uses redirection and it is effective when dealing with the right potential client. If you are a new trainer try the 'redirection' technique until you have learned the more complicated ones mentioned in the following chapter entitled 'closing'.

Keeping the Focus on Price

"Out of the different personal training options, which one are you leaning towards?" **"I want to talk to my husband."** "Did you want to talk to him about the starter package, the accelerated results or the most popular package?" **"I really just want to think about it."** "Did you want to think about the starter package, the accelerated results or the most popular package?" **"I really like the starter package the best but I am not ready to get started until I talk to my husband."** "Did you want to talk to your husband about the price per session or did you want to talk to your husband about the total package price?" **"I want to talk to my husband about the total package price."** "What if I could talk to my boss and get you payment options so that the total package price is more convenient for you, would that make you feel more comfortable?" **"Yes."** If I could talk to my boss and break your package up into payments, would you want to handle your business by cash, check or credit card?" **"Credit card".** "Great and you brought that with you today".

Most objections will center around money. Money is a delicate issue to deal with, so people will avoid talking about it and find other excuses to dwell on. You have seen the excuses above and probably relied on a few yourselves from time to time. Objections are common in this business and you have to learn to overcome them if you are going to be successful.

Chapter 17

CLOSING

I feel that most trainers would agree that the bottom line in a sale is closing the deal. If everything goes great, you've done everything perfectly but you do not close the sale the former is irrelevant {if you fail to close the sale then it is irrelevant as to how well you did}. Nothing was really accomplished, and no money was made. On the other hand, if you do everything wrong, and you still manage to close every sale, then from a financial and results standpoint, you are successful. That is why people who are closers are held in such high regard in our business today. We can compare this to the quarterback who comes in and throws the touchdown pass in the final seconds to win the game or to the pitcher who comes in to closeout the inning. The people who can get it done are the ones who make big money. No matter how you get there, the end result is to win. This is the reason there is such competition and why so many people in the training business, or who are successful in this trade, are ex-athletes who have thrived and excelled when faced with competition.

There are seven steps used by many of the top producers. These are the areas that when focused on will make the difference between closing every package and missing opportunities. This information is the Holy Grail of the personal training business. If you follow the advice, you will see a marked improvement in the area of closing. Although I can offer you ideas on what to say, what you say is not half as important as what you do and how you say it. I have TO'ed thousands of sales, and one of the common things I hear from the new personal trainers is, and I quote, "You just said the exact same thing I said, and they would not join with me. But they joined with you!" I always reply, "Although we said the same words, you and I communicated something totally different."

Remember to practice these seven steps. Reading them will do nothing for you. We do not sell personal training to books; these important steps must be practiced in a role-playing situation. Think of it like a football player who studies the playbook. He must know the playbooks forward and backwards to be successful. But simply knowing the playbook is not enough. He needs to put that knowledge to work during practice and games in order to perfect his craft. He must learn to overcome, improvise, and adapt to many different situations as they happen. You are the quarterback of your career. I will provide the playbook, but you must provide the hard work and dedication it takes to perfect it for you to be successful.

The Seven Steps to Closing

1. Close too often and too early rather than too seldom and too late.

2. You must be assumptive. (Always assume the sale!)

3. Use the force, 93 percent of communication is non-verbal.

4. Mirror and match, people feel comfortable with people who are similar to them.

5. Control the conversation with questions. Answer questions with questions.

6. You must overcome five objections. Most of the sales in the world are made only after the fifth closing attempt.

7. Do not be afraid of silence. After asking any question, be quiet, the first one to talk loses the battle

Close too often and too early rather than too seldom and too late!

You want to close too often and too soon rather than too seldom and too late. You do not want to let the opportunity to close a big package pass you by. Closing too soon rather than too late allows you to get a peek at the person's intentions or to gage their interest level. I always say, relatively early in the close, "Which one of these different package options are you leaning towards?" The potential member will tell you which package he or she is considering, and I quickly say "Welcome to personal training!" It is quick and assumptive, but you may just find the person thanking you and going along with it. If it does not work, the member will usually let you know. It is a gamble worth taking because usually the member will take it as lighthearted and fun and not become too upset. Even if this does happen, you have succeeded in establishing a relaxed situation by making the person laugh. Either way, you are closer to your goal. Here are a couple more examples of questions you can ask to try and close early:

"Were you going to come to your first work out dressed and ready to go? Or were you going to need a locker and a towel?"

I see rookie sales counselors making the following mistake all of the time. "Out of these three package options, which one are you leaning toward?" The member says he likes the starter package. The common mistake that a rookie trainer may make is that they will then ask, "Is the price per session too much or is it the total package price that you are more concerned with?" They have over-anticipated an objection before the member provided one. *Do not do this!* Do not put potentially harmful words in your guest's mouth. The potential client just said they were ready to get started, so do not give them the option to now say it is too much. When faced with this situation, all is not lost. You can still overcome this and meet your objective, but you have made it harder on yourself.

The magic "yes" is not going to fall out of the sky. It just does not happen this way. Very rarely does the person say, "I'll take that package." What you want to do is gain their agreement along the way with questions so they are no longer saying no. If they are not saying no, they must mean yes. Assume the sale; you can never close too early.

You Must be Assumptive!

Being assumptive is probably the best close in sales. Just having an assumptive attitude and saying, "Great, welcome to the club," makes the guest think that it is what everybody does and will simply figure this must be how it works. A lot of the time what we do as personal trainers is offer the prospect an opportunity to haggle by not closing the deal right away while we have the opportunity.

I used to work for a person whose favorite close was to show the prospect the different membership options and say, "You know what? I think this one is best for you." Then he would start filling out the agreement. As soon as the person started to talk, he would ask them a question. "Did you want to pay cash or credit card, your first name, last name, address?" and so on. It was so assumptive that he did not even give the person a chance to think it over. He would just start writing. Many times that closing technique worked. But it takes a lot of time to get to that level unless you are just a natural salesperson.

Use the Force!

Use the force to close the sale. This may sound ridiculous to you as a new trainer but, hey, it worked for Yoda. You may think that selling is just pressuring people and talking them into doing something they do not want to do. Actually, sales have little to do with the words that come from your mouth. Think about this: If you were to go into a dark room with another person, is it or is it not a fact that that a person gives off heat? Is it or is it not a fact that that person gives off energy? Is it or is it not a fact that that person makes sounds when breathing or moving? You can even smell them. With no sight and no words, there are many other forces that can affect communication. Behind words, there are certainly many hidden and not so hidden forces. You can insult someone with a smile and it seems like a joke; joke around with him or her with a frown, and it seems like an insult. Only 5 to 10 percent of the message you send consists of the actual words spoken.

Here are some other factors:

1. The tone of your voice.

2. The speed in which you talk.

3. The proximity between you and your guest.

4. How loud you are.

5. Fear in your voice.

6. Your facial expressions. (Many salespeople blush or make faces, and they are not aware they are doing it!)

7. Eye contact.

8. Ability to remain calm.

9. The speed in which you ask or answer questions.

10. The clarity of your voice.

11. Respect level.

12. Using slang.

I think you get the point. I could go on, but I think you are a newfound believer in the force. As I watch my sales area from 30 feet away, unable to hear any verbal communications, I am aware of what is taking place at each and every table. My trainers or membership counselors will often ask me, "How did you know what was going on?" I simply say, "I do not have to hear what you are saying; I can see everything you are saying just fine."

Mirroring and Matching!

Remember people buy from people they like, and people like people who are similar to them. It is important to adjust style and personality to be in touch with your guest. What does this mean? It means having the ability to change the way you act, talk, and the speed in which you react or walk, everything you do to set your rhythm in sync with the person that you are with. This is not something that I can outline for you. It is not something that is easy to teach. But this is an effective tool.

For Example:

If you have a person who is shy, you cannot be aggressive. If you have a person who walks slowly, you cannot walk fast.

This area of your arsenal can go much deeper. You have to be like a chameleon, which is a lizard that can change its color and/or shape to meet its surroundings.

Lead with Questions!

The person asking the questions is the one in control of the conversation. When it comes down to closing a sale, your guest will ask a lot of questions that they do not really care about hearing the answers to. These are stalling tactics. They are looking for something within your answer that would give them a way out. For instance, you are filling out the paperwork, and Mary asks, "Who teaches your step class?" An inexperienced salesperson might answer, "Oh, it is Jonathan, he is one of our best instructors." Mary says, "I do not feel comfortable doing aerobics in front of a man. I think I will just wait." This exact scenario has taken place right before my eyes numerous times. As you can see, if this question was *deaf-eared*, or answered with a question, this would have never become a problem.

Ask for the Sale Five Times!

One of the most effective turnovers in sales is to "go ask them one more time." The reason is, people can give up or change their mind. Sixty percent of all sales that are made in the world are done so after the fifth closing objection. Count how many objections or concerns you field while you are with your next couple of guests. I bet it is more than just two or three. Here is something to think about while handling these numerous objections:

- If you give up on the first objection (some trainers do) you will miss 90 percent of all sales you could have made if you could have handled the five objections.

• If you give up on the second concern (a lot of trainers do), you will miss 80 percent of all sales you could have made if you could have handled the five objections.

• If you give up on the third concern (most trainers do), you will miss 70 percent of all sales that could have been made if only you could have handled the five objections.

• Give up on the fourth concern (do *you*?), you are missing 60 percent of all the people you could have helped if you just had of asked one more time.

The point is if you do not have the natural ability to help your guests to feel comfortable or to build rapport, or you fail to use the steps outlined in the "overcoming objections" section, you will never be able to get your potential client feeling comfortable enough to the point where you are able to field several objections without offending them. Remember, sometimes you just have to take the long way around. This may mean getting up from the table and clearing the air, or going back out on the workout floor and re-explaining some of the facilities. Change the scenery for a while. Change the entire subject and try talking for a while about something that has nothing to do with joining on a personal training package. If you are too direct, you will never get to objection number five. Number five is the magic number. It separates the men from the boys, the girls from the women.

After Asking Questions, Shut Up!

The reason we ask questions is to give the member the opportunity to think of the answer. If you answer the questions you have asked instead of allowing them to answer for themselves, then you are not letting the guests think on their own and they are certainly not being closed. You must be patient, ask a question and give the guests as much time as they need to answer the question. Once they have answered that question you should be ready with the next question. Do not ever interrupt your guest; the first one to talk loses the battle or in our case (bought it!). Below is an example of a typical situation where you need to ask questions, wait for a response and then be ready for another question.

For Example:

"Mary, why did you come to the club today?" "I want to lose weight." *"Mary, if you do not mind me asking, you look great to me, why did you want to lose weight?"* "I just saw a picture of myself, and I cannot believe how much weight I have gained." *"How did you feel when you saw that picture, Mary?"* "I couldn't believe it! I decided right then and there that tomorrow I was going to lose fifteen pounds." *"Mary, if I could show you the perfect program to help you lose weight and feel great about yourself in the shortest time possible, would you be interested in getting started today?"* "Absolutely!" *"Mary, did you want to go ahead with the package that included our personal training and nutrition or would you just prefer to go with our basic training program today?"* "I will take the trainer and the nutrition." *"Welcome to the club!"*

Closing Types:

The Verbal Closing: "If I could, would you"

Of all the closes I can think of, this one is still one of the best. It is, "If I could, would you…" This means that if I could get that for you today would you want to get started. You always want to be two steps ahead of the other salespeople.

For Example:

"You know, we used to have this program. I do not know if I can still get it for you, but I can talk to my manager. I do not know if he will go for it, but if I could *talk to him and see if I could get that for you,* would you *be interested in getting started today?"*

In many cases you will show the potential client your training options and they will say they want to think about it. What you need to do is mention the package that was just available, but has since expired. Then you can offer the "if I could, would you" close.

The "If I could would you!"

"Out of the different personal training packages which one are you leaning towards" **"I need to think about it!"** "I can understand you want to think about it but if you were to pick one, which one would it be?" **"Probably the middle one."** "You know we had a special package option for that particular program, but it has expired! Earlier today my boss authorized one of these for one of our VIP members, if I could go talk to my boss and get this kind of option would you be interested. **"What was the special price?"** "It was 16 sessions at $40 per session. I could ask my boss. I'm not making any promises but the worst thing he can do is say no?" **"Go ask?"** "If my boss says yes how will pay cash or credit card?" **"Cash!"** "And you brought that with you today"?

Two sales, One guest

This close I am going to tell you in story form. I see so many personal trainers make the mistake of not taking the opportunity of turning one sale into two or three sales. This happens because of a very simple reason: They never ask for it. I travel back and forth from the United States to Taiwan on a regular basis. Since I live in Nevada, I usually have a lay over in San Francisco. There is a young boy there who is great at shining shoes. He is a master at his trade. He puts a lot of flare into the art of shoe shining. As I arrive at the San Francisco Airport, I see that he is working. I go over to him and ask him how much it is for a shoeshine. He replies by saying, "All of the other shine boys charge $2.50. If you want a shine from me, it is going to cost you $3. It is a little more but I guarantee you, you will know where that extra 50 cents went." Then he turns his eyes down towards my shoes, and he says, "Those look like a pair of expensive shoes." I say, "Yes, they are. They cost a lot of money." Then he replies to me, "Why don't you buy a cheaper pair of shoes, like ones from discount shoe stores?" I respond by saying, "Quality is important to me. I believe you get what you pay for." He looks me in the eyes, smiles, and responds by saying, "Then I guess you want to have your shoes shined by me." I smile and take a seat in the chair. He opens up his box and starts to shine my shoes. Each time the towel hits my shoes, it makes a popping sound. He has perfected this trick over the thousands of shoes he must have polished. He spins the towel and hums and appears as if he is singing a song with the friction and popping coming from the towel. He then looks down at the bottom of my shoes and says to me, "These are Italian leather shoes, and I must admit they are some of the nicest I have ever seen." As he comes to the finish, I can see he has done an excellent job shining my shoes. He looks at me and he says, "You know I have something in my box that they made just for expensive Italian shoes just like these. It may cost you 50 cents more, but your shoeshine will last twice as long. Do you want to go with the Italian lotion or did you just want me to finish up with the cheap stuff?" By now, I am sure you can guess my answer. Just by the way that he phrased his questions and the confidence he did it with, I was sold. A professional salesman being closed by a boy. He then does something that most experienced salespeople often forget to do. He asks me how long my lay over will be. I respond by saying that I will be in the airport for another couple of hours before taking off for my home. He then asks me if I have to dress up for work every day. I respond by saying, "Yes, unfortunately, I have to wear a suit and tie to work." The boy then responds by saying, "Do you wear the same pair of shoes every day?" I say, "No, I have different colored shoes for the different suits that I wear." As I see the wheels in his head turning, he looks at me and says, "If you have other shoes with you, I will be willing to shine them as well. Not only that, but I will be willing to put the expensive Italian lotion on them for free, sound fair?" Without giving me the time to respond, he follows up by saying, "Leave your shoes here for me, go grab something to eat, and they will be ready in 20 minutes." Whether I say yes or no is not the point, the point is that he asked. He turns one sale into three, and he adds 50 cents with the lotion. I am sure that not every person says yes, but if

25 percent of the people do, he increases his sales by a large percentage. Do not forget to *up-sell*. Who says you can't learn a lot from a child?

Are you aware of the fact that McDonald's Corp. increased their sales 25 percent by simply asking one question: "Would you like fries or a coke with that?" They took it even one step further by asking people if they would like to "Super Size" their fries and cokes. They take the sale one step further by changing their menus from having all the different foods listed on the menu to having meal deals on the menu. Instead of having to pick just the hamburger or just the french-fries, they all come together in a meal for one low price.

The Lost Sale Close

The *lost sale* close is one you can use when your potential client is in the parking lot. It is a last ditch effort when everything else has failed. It starts with first letting the member know that you are aware they are not going to join on a package today but you were just letting them know that this is how you earn a living. Tell them that their feedback is important to you improving your craft and ask them some questions.

For Example:

"What did I do wrong? I must have done something wrong? I can't help anyone get started. I just want to help people and no one wants to help themselves. Is it me? Is something wrong with me? Did I do something to offend you? Maybe I am just not cut out to help people. Maybe those other used car salesmen inside were right. Maybe I should quit being so nice and just start taking people's money. Forget about their goals and dreams."

I know, I know, it is a pretty low move. It is also pretty shameless, but believe it or not, this method does work from time to time. Hopefully you do not find yourself in any situations where you have to resort to a tactic like this. If you do find yourself in that situation, it is good to have a script ready.

Keeping the Focus on Price

"Out of the different personal training options, which one are you leaning toward?" "**I want to think about it.**" "Did you want to think about the starter package, the accelerated results or the most popular package?" "**I really just want to think about it.**" "Did you want to think about the starter package, the accelerated results or the just the most popular package?" "**I really like the starter package the best but I am not ready to get started until I talk to my husband.**" "Did you want to talk to your husband about the price per session or did you want to talk to your husband about the total package price?" "**I want to talk to my husband about the total package price.**" "What if I could talk to my boss and get you payment options so that the total package price is more convenient for you, would that make you feel more comfortable?" "**Yes.**" If I could talk to my boss and break your package up into payments, would you want to handle your business by cash or credit card?" "**Credit card**". "You brought that with you today?"

The Alternate Choice

The *alternate choice* is what we do when we show the member all of the different package options and then say, "Would you want to go with option one or would you prefer option two? Out of the different options which one are you leaning toward? Did you want to start today or would tomorrow be better for you? Do you want your membership with a male trainer or a female trainer?" The alternate choice is a simple and effective close. In sales, you will learn that if you give somebody two choices they are going to take one of them. "Did you want to go with cash, check or credit card?" It has been around forever and works in all types of businesses. Learn it and get used to it because you will see that you will probably use this close as much as, if not more than any other.

The Ben Franklin Close

This close is especially good for closing a personal training package. This close involves developing a plus *vs.* minus system. This close does not necessarily have to be a health club close as it can be used for anything that you are trying to sell. What really matters is that you have the positives and the negatives of why the potential client should make a decision. It is very effective but do not be afraid if it takes a while as you may have to go through a little bit of a process in order to make this happen.

Ben Franklin, one of our countries founders had to make a number of complicated decisions, fortunately for us, he was a smart man. Whenever Ben Franklin had to make a difficult decision he would list the positives and the negatives of why he should make that decision. He would make a list of all the reasons why he should do it and all the reasons why he should not do it. Based on the positives against the negatives, he would weigh it out and decide if he should make the decision or wait for a while before deciding. If the positives outweighed the negatives, he would make that decision and *vice versa*. If there were a clear distinction between the two then he would choose the one with the most points in its favor, be it positive or negative.

It is really quite simple, all you need to do is write the answers to questions given by the customer onto a piece of paper. Title one side of the paper, *Positives* and the other side of the paper, *Negatives*. Ask the customer, "What positives do you think will come from you becoming more healthy and losing weight?" The answers will vary and include such positives as health, looking good, lower blood pressure, feeling better, strengthen the heart, increased energy and stamina, and so on. If they do not come up with enough give them a couple of more positives so you can fill up that column. Do not give them too many because you want them to see their answers on the paper. After writing down about ten to twelve positives, move over to the negatives. Ask the customer, "What are some of the negatives you can see as a result of getting in shape and improving your health?" The funny thing about the question is that there is no acceptable answer to it.

Whatever you do, do not help them fill out this side of the paper, they will have a hard enough time finding any answers so do not help them. You will receive answers such as, "I don't have the time" or "I don't have the money," two of the easiest objections to overcome. That is about it. You have not only showed them that the positives outweigh the negatives, you have also uncovered a couple of objections. Your next step is to read back all of the positives and then the negatives. Your closing question will be something like, "Mary, wouldn't you agree that sacrificing an average of one hour of your time and few bucks is a small price to pay to be able to live longer, look better, have more energy, lower you blood pressure, sleep better, and more?" (Simply read back their positives.)

You have now made it obvious that their objections have been squashed underneath the pressure of all of the positives they are going to receive. You have built value within the product and shown that they need to listen to you in order to achieve their goals, that the only way to get all of the positives is to get started on the program. Once they have seen that, they find it hard to say no because it is simply not a logical answer. It takes a little longer than some of the other closes but it is well worth it.

Motivational Speaker

"Mary, last week I went to a seminar featuring a motivational speaker. He explained that the reason people are unhappy with their life is that they spend a lot of time and energy worrying about the little things and they fail to take care of the big things. He said and I think that you will agree, that there are four major areas in your life and if you take care of these four areas, then the rest of your life will be more enjoyable. They include your relationships (friends, family, and loved ones), financial stability, spirituality, and your health. He explained that these four things affected each other. Having no friends or family could affect your health. Having poor health could affect your job. Having no spirituality could affect your ability to care or have a meaning in life. Now, Mary, I do not know if the motivational speaker was right or wrong, but I think you would agree with me that without your health, nothing else really matters."

The Negative Take-Away Close

I found that this close works extremely well with a person that shows little interest or emotion. You have to find something in this individual that will stimulate action. I found that sometimes the only way to do this is by taking something away. You may find that your guest says that they are not really interested in getting started on a package. They are not really interested in exercise, and they never thought about working out before. It is going to be hard for you to gain commitment if you cannot get your guest's attention. You may simply state that it is okay and that even if they wanted to get started on a package today it would be impossible for you to sign them up. Tell them that unfortunately, at this time, the club is full of members that care about being healthy. You may recommend putting them on a waiting list and giving them a call back when there is an opening for you to take more clients. This may spark something in them that makes them want something they cannot have. The guest may be using this technique to try to get you to beg them to get started. When you do not show interest, they will be surprised. This will cause them to loosen up on their objections and force him or her to show an interest in order to get what you will not give him or her. In many cases the prospective client will try to buy their way through the waiting list.

Magic Potion

I use this close quite often for people who believe that there are shortcuts to becoming healthy. Trendy diets, weight loss retreats, starving, steroids, all of these are worthless without exercise and a good diet and yet people still waste their time trying them. You have to use a little bit of imagination and have a fairly good rapport with your guest. Ask your guest to think of a time when they were in the best shape of their life. Make them think about the time when they felt great, looked great, and people would comment on their accomplishments. Then pick up a cup or a bottle of white out and look at the guest and say, "What if I had a magic potion, that you could drink and when you awoke the following morning you would have the perfect body? If I had a potion like that, how much do you think I would be able to sell it for?" You can ask your guest, "If I had a potion like that, how much will you be willing to pay for it?" Your guest may respond by saying, "That would be priceless. You can sell it for any amount." I respond by saying, "So you would agree that your body is also priceless? You and I both know there is no quick fix, there is no magic potion. Believe me, if there was, Oprah Winfrey the richest woman in the country would not be overweight. The only way for you to have the perfect body is for you to adjust your lifestyle to include your priceless body."

The Magic Potion close works to get the client to understand that there is no easy way to losing weight and maintaining their health. This close must only be done with those clients with whom you have built a strong rapport. If you try it with someone who you do not have a good rapport with, they will not follow along and will miss the point of the presentation.

The Only Car You Will Ever Have

When I first started in sales, this close was one used by a good friend of mine. Personally, I have never used it, but it seemed to work very well for him. He would simply ask the guest a series of questions to make the guest realize how important health and fitness was. He would compare the person's body to an automobile. He would state, "John, I want you to imagine, you are living in a foreign country. And in this country, there is a rule; the rule is that you are only going to have one automobile to last for your entire lifetime. The rule is put in place to teach people to take care of things and be responsible. On your 21st birthday, you are given your one automobile to have for your lifetime. Would you change the oil in your

automobile? Would you keep your automobile clean? Wou~
the best gasoline in it? Would you put the protection on the ru~~
and leather? I am sure you would agree with me, if you were only
going to have one automobile for the rest of your life, one of your
highest priorities would be to take care of it. Wouldn't you agree?
John, the reason I ask you these questions is in relation to your body.
You only get one body; you will never ever have a chance to get
another one. I think you would agree that having one body is more
important than having one car."

This is a very successful close. The entire time you are working
to gain the agreement of your guest. Once they have realized the
point or the correlation between the story and their body, it becomes
almost irrational for them to say no. This must only be done if you
have built a strong rapport with the client. If you do not, much like
the Magic Potion close, they will not gain the significance of it.

Benefits Not Bashing

One of the most important techniques used in sales today is focusing on the benefits. How is our product going to benefit the
customer? Why it is important for the customer to have the product?
Why does the customer need it? How does our product differ from
other products? All of these questions need to be addressed before
you are going to make a successful sale. The goal is to cut down on
everything but the pure benefits. It is important to use our three-step
method, statement of fact, two to three questions and a tie-down.

For Example:

"*John, now I have explained the benefits of our personal training program, I think you would agree that no other trainer can offer
you a program to compare with mine.*" It is important not to knock
other trainers; it can ruin your credibility. When a guest talks about
the benefits of another trainer, I simply agree and say "*John, Tommy
is a very nice trainer, and I think you would agree that he has a very
good price. But what I would like to do is take a moment of your time
to tell you the benefits of my program, as well as the best price, and*

let you make the decision for yourself, sound fair?"

By doing this, you are keeping the member interested in your abilities. You are allowing them to make their own decision but asking them in a way that only the answer "yes" will benefit them. Remember, you are there to make them happy. If you are looking out for their interests and trying to find benefits for them, they will appreciate it and you will have a stronger rapport.

The "Thinking About It" Close

This objection is at the tip of every customer's tongue if they are going to give one. If a person gives you this objection, they are in a situation where they are searching for a way out of committing, most likely to try to avoid spending money. It is what we call a "secondary objection" because it is often used to hide another. When the situation arises, stay calm and remember this close.

For Example:

"I can understand you want to think about it. Other people have felt the same way that you feel. What we have found is that most people have already thought of everything there is to think about. Then what ends up happening is you go home, you walk towards the door, you pick up your mail, and you start thinking about the bills you have to pay. You go in and listen to your answering machine, turn on the TV, get busy with the dinner and kids. One thing leads to another, and all of a sudden, it is six months down the road, and you really have not gotten back around to doing what you originally had the best intentions of doing today. Every morning we wake up and have the best intentions of doing all of the things that are going to make our life better. It just seems by noon, or half way through the day, our mind has tricked our bodies into making the wrong decision, into procrastinating, waiting, or putting it off until tomorrow. I think you would agree, that the time is right, and now is the time. What better place to think about it? You have all the information that you need on the table, you have an environment that is free from distraction, and you have me here to answer all of your questions."

It is quite a bit to remember but it is the only close you are going to need in this situation. You will find that people will make objections, such as this one, just because they are afraid to commit to anything. When they are in a situation where they cannot find anything they truly object to, they will fall back on their old-reliable "I want to think about it."

The "What about this? What about that? What if I could?" Close

I have found that the most effective close is just offering the guest different options until you find one that works for them. Most of the time, your guest is not going to tell you the real reason as to why they are not getting started. They will come up with objections instead of telling you the real reason they are not joining the club is that you, the professional, have not yet found a training option to fit their needs. I read a great book about sales not too far back that really opened my eyes. Two salesmen wrote this book, and it only contained facts and figures on what motivated people to make a purchase.

They put hidden cameras in sales offices all over the world and studied what the key points involved in the person's final decisions were. More interestingly to me was when they focused on what the different salespeople did in different situations when confronted with different objections. The two biggest factors were No. 1, the salesperson never asked for the sale, and No. 2, they could not find an option that met the customer's needs. Many salespeople today cannot close a sale because they do not understand the fact that the one or two options that they are offering are not working for the customer.

For Example:

"Mary, this package option includes a one time total investment of 500 dollars, leaving your balance investment at only $250." "I need to think about it." "Mary, let me ask you a question, is taking

care of your package in full an option for you?" "I still want to try it first." *"Mary, what if I could get you a smaller package that would give you an opportunity to try the training program, as well as a little more time to see the benefits exercise will have on you?"* "That sounds a little better." *"I have a 3session option for $120 and I have 5 session option for $200. Both of them would give you some time to see changes in your body. At the end of that your package will expire. If you decide you like the program, and you are seeing results we could talk about a longer term commitment. I think this may answer all of your concerns. Out of option 1 and option 2, which one would you be leaning towards?"* "Option 2." *"Mary, welcome to the one on one training program. Your address? Phone number? Would you be handling your membership by cash, check or credit card?"* "Credit card." *"And you brought that with you today?"*

The example I have given above shows that Mary really did want to get started. I simply had to find a package option that elevated her concerns and met her needs. This is very common in our business. Many times it is not that the guest does not want to enroll, it is that the guest has not seen anything that they really feel comfortable with. The reason most successful trainers and clubs have multiple package options is so they can tailor them to suit many different people and their individual needs. It is your job to find the best one for each situation.

The "Just Do It" Close

I hate to say it, but sometimes just saying the words, *"Oh, come on, just do it!"* will be motivation enough for some people to enroll. I do not know why this works, but it does. I do not know how many times this close has been used in high schools to get an under-aged kid to drink his first beer. The words, *"Oh, come on, just do it!"* work.

You must have a good rapport with your guest to use this one. It is playful, yet effective. Many people simply need to have somebody there to give them that extra shove to get them going.

My Grandma Close

This close works very well with senior citizens and long-time procrastinators. You will often find yourself unable to get older people to even answer any of the questions. When this happens, I change gears and go from sales mode to story mode. I simply sit down at the table and say, "*John, I know that you are not interested in making a decision today. You know there is a little story I would like to tell you, it would only take a minute of your time if you do not mind. I wanted to tell you the reason I had for getting into this business. When I was in my early 20s, I was still very active in sports and was very serious about making it to the club on the daily basis. At the time, I was concerned with looking great and feeling great and I truly could not understand why anyone would choose to not exercise. At that time, I had a grandmother who was in her early 60's, and was in pretty poor physical condition. She worked long hours; her diet included a steady supply of cheese, chips, coffee, cigarettes and aspirin. Several times a week, I would stop by her house on my way to the gym and raid her refrigerator. On my way out, I would ask her, 'Grandma, why don't you go to the gym with me today? There are lots of other people there just like you, and they feel great about their exercise programs.' She would always respond by saying, 'I am busy', or 'Not today, I will go with you tomorrow.' She would give me every excuse in the book. As the years went by, she seemed to have less energy, more health problems, and an overall, lackluster outlook on life. So finally one day, I walked in her house, I put her in a headlock, I literally dragged her, kicking and scratching into the gym with me. After taking a 15-minute swim and some light resistance training, my grandmother had seemed to be reborn. She spoke to some of the other seniors in the club, and they gave her a schedule for the senior classes. After leaving the facility, she felt energy and vigor that she had not felt in years. My grandmother has continued on an exercise program three days a week for the past seven years. If you were to ask her about her physical condition, she would tell you she feels better at 70 than she felt at 40. John, if I let you leave the club today with out a training package, I would be going against everything that my grandmother believes was the best decision she ever made. She still reminds me of the day that I dragged her to the car and dragged her into the club, and it reminds me of the joy of helping someone, like yourself, do what you know you should do right now!"*

Overcoming Objections

I am going to give you two or more ways to overcome each of the objections.

"Spouse (I want to talk husband or wife, Mom or dad.")

Option 1

"I want to talk to my wife" "you want to talk to your wife?" "Yes we have an agreement whenever we do anything in regard to money we talk it over!" "I can understand that I am married too and this is a big decision. I know you wouldn't even be considering talking to your wife if you weren't **very** serious. Let me ask you one question other than talking to your wife is there any thing else holding you back from getting started to day?" "No." "Let me ask you this Larry, if the personal training package was three dollars a session would you be able to make a decision today with out your wife." "Yes." "So you can spend money without talking to your wife, just not a lot of money, is it the price per session or the total package price that is too much." "It is the total package price!" "So if I could talk to my boss and get your package price reserved with a small deposit and you could go home and talk to your wife would that work for you?" "Yes." "How much could you put down today to hold this price?" "Half." "Okay Larry let me go talk to my boss." "Larry how do you normally handle your business, cash check or credit card?" "Credit card." "You brought that with you today?"

Option 2

You go call your husband and see if he will let you purchase the package, and I will call my wife and see if it is okay for me to sell the package to you."

Option 3

"Your wife is going to say no?" "No, my wife isn't going to say no." "Well, she doesn't care, she probably won't want you to spend money." "Is she is going say yes?" "If you are so sure your wife will say yes, then you really don't still need to ask her?"

Option 4

"Your body has nothing to do with any other person other than you. Your husband/wife cannot workout for you or tell you not to work out. Your body is yours, and it is 100 percent your decision. Buying a car or a house is different, because it is communal property. Your body belongs to you and it is your decision if you want to be healthier or feel good about the way you look. No other person can make that decision, wouldn't you agree?"

"My friend is going to train me."

Option 1

I understand that you have a lot of confidence in your friend. I think you would agree with me when I say that going through a couple of personal training sessions can give you a better understanding of whether or not your friend has a training program that can get you the results that you are looking for.

Option 2

I appreciate the fact that you feel that your friend is a great exercise enthusiast. I should also remind you that our company policy requires all the trainers to have a certification and insurance coverage to operate in this facility.

"I don't have time"

Option 1

I usually quickly respond by saying, "you don't have time not to!"

Option 2

John, you have already made an incredible investment in regards to the time and amount of money that you have put aside for exercise, if time is a concern, I can show you that I specialize in programs that give you more results in less time. Now you will have more time.

"I want to try it on my own"
Option 1

John, I understand that you want to try it on your own, I also understand that you have had success in the past. Exercise is a relatively new concept and fitness in regards to what works and what does not. Some of the new information that I have to offer can help you get results quicker and easier and I'm sure if you are like everyone else, you would like to make your workouts quicker, easier, and more effective.

Option 2

John, when I was in my early 20's, I decided to take up golf. I went out and bought an expensive set of golf clubs, and despite the pro shop advice, I refused having a pro give me some pointers. In time, I developed a very interesting new system for making the ball curve when I hit it. When I finally decided to go in and see a professional to make an adjustment, it was extremely difficult for me to change my bad habits. If I had learned to play golf the right way in the beginning, I would have been well adjusted by this time. I implore you not to make the same mistake or pick-up the same bad habits that I did.

"I want to think about it"
Option 1

"I can give you three days to shop around. If for any reason you find any other product that offers better reliability or you like better, come back to get a full refund, and I can still give you a discount by starting today. There is nothing to lose!"

Option 2

"Mr. Prospect, you want to think about it? I can understand you want to think about it. I understand how you feel. Other people have felt the same way, but what we have found is that by joining on a package today, it will be the best decision you will ever make in your life. Other than thinking about it, is there anything else to stop you from joining on a package today?" "No." "May I ask you a question? How many days are you going to need to think about?" "Two days." "What if I could give you two days to think about it, and still give you a discount on your package by starting up today? I could give you a discount today and you would have three days to decide to keep your training package or get a refund. Sound fair?"

Option 3

If it is over the telephone: "I want you to go to all the other stores in town, make sure you take notes about the different price options and services that are provided by the other retailers. Then, I want you to come to our office with the information. I will prove to you that our business can beat any other business when it comes to the services that we provide. Not only that, but I will also beat any businesses price. I think you would agree this is the right way to make the most educated decision. Would morning or evening be best for you?"

"Group/friends" "I have a friend and we want to workout together."

Option 1

It is true working out with a friend can offer some great benefits, in most cases I found that in modern day society, with jobs and families, and all the things going on, sometimes being consistent with a partner can be impossible. Why don't we get you started with a 3-session package, and if your friend is interested, they can join us during our sessions.

Option 2

Not only do I specialize in 1-on-1 personal training and nutrition, but I also specialize in group training sessions. If you would be interested, I might be able to talk to my boss and include a program that would teach you and your friend how to train together and how to accomplish your goals in the shortest amount of time possible. If I can talk to my boss and teach you and your friend how to benefit from group training, how would you handle your business: cash, credit card, or check?

"It's too expensive."

Option 1

You can break it down to the ridiculous, most of the time it will be. *"Your membership is $20 per month, how much too much is it?"* "It is $5 too much." *"So $5 is stopping you from joining the club today?"* "Yes." *"Five dollars divided by 30 days equals 16 cents per day, so 16 cents per day is stopping you from becoming healthier? Don't you think your health and happiness is worth 16 cents per day?"*

Option 2

"It's too expensive" is the best objection we can get. Out of all of the other objections, it is truly the one we have the most control over. We cannot control what their husbands are going to say, cannot control how convenient the club is for them. But we certainly have control over different personal training package options and prices available to them. You must learn how to handle this objection with many different tactics. If you do not, you will lose a large number of potential sales. You are going to hear it, so you better start practicing for it.

Option 3

"Out of the different personal training options, which one are you leaning toward?" "it's too expensive." "Was it the starter package, the accelerated results or the most popular package that was a little more than you were looking to spend?" **"I really just think that it is a little out of my price range."** "Which one of the packages is a little bit too much, the starter package, the accelerated results or the just the most popular package?" **"I really like the starter package the best but I am not ready to get started until I talk to**

my husband." "Did you want to talk to your husband about the price per session or did you want to talk to your husband about the total package price?" **"I want to talk to my husband about the total package price."** "What if I could talk to my boss and get you payment options so that the total package price is more convenient for you, would that make you feel more comfortable?" **"Yes."** If I could talk to my boss and break your package up into payments, would you want to handle your business by cash or credit card?" **"Credit card".** "You brought that with you today".

You will get objections, everybody does. The best are the ones who have enough in their arsenal to overcome a variety of different objections and attitudes with a variety of different tactics and personalities. If you want to be the best, you must learn to overcome objections. The few that I have detailed for you will be the most common. Learn them, overcome them, and be the best.

Chapter 18

MY FIRST EXPERIENCE AS A TRAINER AND THE JAKE SEINFELD STORY

As a new personal trainer, you will spend many hours studying detailed exercise physiology. You may spend a substantial amount of time learning the intricate functions of the human body. As your education progresses you will learn how to schedule and juggle your different workout routines. After completing these difficult tasks, you will have an opportunity to go out into the real world. For most trainers this is the time when you may begin to observe your educational shortcomings and the answers during this difficult time may be rather elusive.

When I was a young student studying to get my degree, I had made a decision that after I completed my education that I would go in to an exercise or fitness type of career field. After studying for years and learning everything I possibly could about my field, I found myself getting ready to enter the working world. After doing some research, I found that the best fit for me would be working for a large health club organization, one that had high volume, a good earning potential, the possibility of getting promoted and different locations in different cities. The most important aspect of working for a larger and more seasoned organization would come in the form of a comprehensive training program. When I started the process of interviewing and applying for different companies, the main focus of the employer had little to do with my educational background; in fact it seemed almost irrelevant. Some of the questions that were coming out of the mouths of the potential employers were rather shocking. The first place I went to apply was a chiropractor and rehab center that had sort of a fitness style health club in the back. It was a well known and established and had a good reputation. I had a chance to meet with one of the partners and he told me that all the trainers had great earning potential. The only problem came from the fact that the job paid zero base salary and expected the trainers to work for free until they had built a certain number of clients. Not only was this odd to me, but the clinic also required that we pay for our own advertisements. The partner also stated that we were not allowed to use their customers as new clients! After determining this was not the best option for me, and feeling this was just an odd system. I decided to go to one of the large well-known health club chains. After going through an initial interview process with the head personal trainer, I then had an opportunity to meet with the regional fitness director. The first words out of the director's mouth was, **"Sell Me Personal Training."** I explained that I had not gone through an official sales training courses and I was not particularly interested in becoming a sales person. The regional training director told me that in a health club, every employee in every department must have the ability to sell. After going to several interviews, I found that all of the different organizations that I was trying to approach had one thing in common, "Making Money." After dedicating several weeks, and many frustrating hours, toward the grueling task of getting someone to believe that I could help health club members get results, I determined that maybe being a personal trainer was not something that was going to be in my future.

Upset and a little frustrated and maybe feeling like it was time to give up, I decided to go back and double check the agenda and text material that had been such an intricate part of my learning process. Maybe I was sick the week the certification program covered selling. Maybe I was not paying attention when the teacher talked about the needs and wants of future employers. After spending significant time on research, I realized the structure for selling and retaining or even acquiring new clients simply wasn't present in any of the training material that I was provided. Why would an organization dedicated to teaching such an honorable trade pay absolutely no attention whatsoever on how to make money or how to get a job. I decided that drastic times called for drastic measures. I had a close friend who had worked in the executive level of a large health club organization. He had since moved on to other things, but had maintained a great reputation for being a top producer in the health club business and was still highly respected. I asked if we could meet and if he would assist me by answering some of the questions that I thought would help me in my quest to find out how these organizations functioned.

"Why don't other professionals such as physical therapist or chiropractors have to sell?" "Who told you those guys don't have to sell? The main difference between the chiropractors that make 100,000 and the one that make 30,000 is their ability to sell. Most of those guys don't even make it through their first year because they give up when faced with what you are going through right now."

"Why do the trainers have to sell?" "It may not be that they want you to be a great salesman, they just want to know that you are open to the fact that money is an important part of any business. A health club or rehabilitation center is a business first and foremost. Nobody can offer a business service if they can't pay their electricity bill. Would you work for free?" I responded by saying, "of course not!" This answer really made sense to me"

"Why is selling such a high priority?" "Selling is such a high priority for the company because of the following factors. This is a fitness center and the goal of the fitness center is the same as those of the guest or the members it is to get results. It is to get bigger, better, faster, and stronger. This is what kind of employees they are looking for; they want to know how you can help each and every member get results. Can you get a member results in 1 or 2 sessions? Can you get a member results if you can't get them to show up to their sessions. Can you get a client results if you can't get them to change their poor life style? Can you get a member results if you can't get them to start working out? You have to be able to sell every aspect of fitness or procrastination will win."

"Why do these companies pay so little as a base salary and such a high commission?"

"In a health club most people that work with trainers are doing so because they are not self motivated or because they want someone who will push them. Most of these individuals will not make the initial move when it comes to asking for the service. In most cases, even if they do ask they will procrastinate about getting started without a little push. The club benefits the most from members that get results and this may not happen if the member is not encouraged by the trainer to get started on the training program. The commission pay system rewards trainers that actively recruit new clients and work with members to accomplish their goals. Also, if the club pays a percentage the system will be fair and even in regards to the amount of money coming in and the amount of money being paid out." Everything seemed clearer to me now.

"Why didn't the schools teach you how to get a job or how to sell?"

"The schools are a business first and the most important thing for them is to get students to pay the fee for completing the class, when you pay they make money. If the schools focused on selling or the hardships of clients not showing up for their 5am appointments a good percentage of the students would not complete the course. Lets face it, the realities of the business world are not always pleasant."

He went on to say, "listen I don't have all the answers and being a trainer is not just fun and games. You will have days just like in any job where things will not fall your way. You will have days where you boss will ride you for sales, you will have days where all your clients will flake out, and days where no one will buy what you are selling, you may even have your favorite client tell you that they are in love with you. Be aware that you are dealing with people and be prepared for all the problems that can come with that. My best advice to you is for you to understand that companies need people like you, and you are a very valuable resource. Go to the establishment that you think will be right for you, talk to some of the trainers and find out if the organization fits in with what you are looking for. You must understand that most large companies have put a substantial amount of time in to the systems that they trust in and use. They are looking for motivated individuals that will learn these systems, perfect them, and then take them to new levels once they have been fully absorbed. Be open to working hard at first and believing in company values, once that has been accomplished you can have your own ideas about how to run a large club training department. **Maybe someday you will be writing the courses for the future training classes.**"

After meeting with my friend, I felt that most of what he had said made sense. I certainly felt that after the time and effort I had put into becoming a personal trainer, it was not in my personality type to just give up and throw all that education and hard work down the drain. I decided that it was time for me to confront my fears and find out everything I could about being a personal trainer in the real world.

The first thing I wanted to know is why and how personal training became the business it is today. As far as I could tell from my research, coaching in some form or another had been around since the beginning of organized sports. In the incredible hulks early days, the movie :Pumping Iron", shows Big Lou being coached by his father whereas Arnold Schwarzenegger, on his rise to super stardom, is coached by the incredible Joe Wieder. I really found that this form of working with a coach had not really reached the masses or at least for the average blue collar paid individual until recently. As far as my research could tell me, the trend of having a personal trainer started in Hollywood, of all places there was a story of a young overweight and gullible Jewish boy who had grown up in a poor neighborhood of New York.

He was mocked and ridiculed which led him to start exercising and lifting weights as a teenager. He soon decided that he wanted to become a body builder like his icon peers from "Pumping Iron." Jake was taking the transformation of his body very seriously and he realized that if he wanted to progress to the next level, he had to travel to Los Angeles, California, the birthplace of bodybuilding. After arriving in the body building Mecca of Venice Beach, Jake realized that there was more to being a professional body builder than just lifting weights. After learning some long hard facts and milling them over, he made a decision that the drugs involved in creating the type of body to win and compete at this level would go against his family's beliefs. Jake decided that just because he was unable to pursue a career as a professional body builder that there were still other opportunities that could be fulfilled in the arena of exercise and fitness.

His first job was working in a local fitness center as a front desk counter person for a free membership and to help cover his rent. He had only worked in the position for a short time when a gentleman by the name of Frances approached him. The man asked Jake a question that may have changed the world of fitness forever. "Would you be interested in offering some of your fitness expertise or techniques to help my overweight daughter?" Jake decided based on the fact that he was in desperate need of money that he would be interested in this business opportunity. Other members in the club told Jake that this person was some kind of famous producer in the movie business and that his daughter was kind of strange. The overall member consensus was that Jake would never accomplish the difficult feat requested by the father. One of the biggest problems with the unique offer was that Jake was required to train Francis's daughter at their home.

The other problem came from the fact that the home did not offer any modern fitness equipment. Jake being the friendly, outgoing person that he was, was not discouraged and took the job very seriously. The task was not an easy one and most of the exercise was done using household equipment such as: a broomstick and a kitchen chair. The reason why Jake was able to perform such an incredible feat came from the simple fact that when he was younger and money was scarce he had trained himself using some of these same techniques.

News quickly spread as the person that Jake Seinfeld was training was Francis Ford Copella's daughter and the movie he was preparing her for was "The Godfather 3". The young girl that had been known around town for being the fat girl daughter of a famous movie producer had now become the star sex symbol in an academy award-winning movie. The news of Jake's personal training success traveled like wildfire through the who's who of Hollywood.

Soon many of Hollywood's elite actors and actresses were using this newfound system for getting optimal results in a fitness center. Jake trained stars like "Steven Spielberg," "Harrison Ford," and many other well-known movie icons. Soon everyone in Hollywood was talking about experiencing incredible success with the help of his or her personal trainer. Hollywood stars could afford to have a personal trainer, but it would take some time and a considerable amount of effort to convince the average working class citizens to spend their hard earned dollars on one-on-one sessions.

My first experience in the world of selling fitness came from working in a large health club chain as a membership counselor although I was more interested in being a trainer at the time and had been involved in sports just about every waking day of my life. At that time selling memberships was the position they had open so I took it, anything to get your foot in the door. Membership selling was just starting to become something of an art form. Something that only a very few incredibly skilled and highly trained individuals were able to do well. At the time, there were only a couple of companies that had more than ten or so clubs. Systems had not yet been standardized and most health club chains had just recently started to develop a culture that could produce any substantial profits. This was the era that fitness centers went from business to big business!

Before that, owning a gym was really only for people who wanted to exercise and did not care about offering quality equipment or services, this suicidal proprietor could never dream of producing a living. During this time, most health clubs only sold a couple items such as t-shirts and memberships. Personal training was something that was very rare, used mainly in a rehab situation or by some incredibly rich starlet. The health club business had gone through a sort of metamorphous in regard to the fact that they had discovered EFT. This was a huge breakthrough that created a reoccurring long-term income from a business that had a hard time collecting payment. It was also a time when investors started to see the light on the possibilities of taking a small business and turning it into an anchor institution that would be needed by the average American. This was also the time when the computer became the norm in the average business or household. For the first time people had discovered how to do away with most of the manual labor that had been commonplace in keeping people fit. To be honest, the computer industry was the main factor for the increasing obesity of the average American.

As the health club industry experienced a huge increase in usage, it became evident that people were beginning to realize that this was something that was growing into a necessity. As the business grew, it also matured into well defined and incredibly effective sales and marketing systems. As these systems were put into place, they were tested, tried, and improved by the people in the trenches, the gifted individuals who had spent many years developing a system that could work in a health club. These systems were developed from a business that had everything going against it and was still able to create an income. Selling fitness is unlike any other retail product. You have to think of the customer as an addict. This is the thing that most individuals don't understand about the business.

When a person wants something, they go out and they buy it. When a person wants to change their lifestyle, they will never do it unless someone helps them, the reason most addicts never recover is because they don't have the willpower to do it on their own. Poor lifestyle addicts are begging for relief, but they are not going to ask you to take away their best friend (poor lifestyle). I mean think about it, what person wants to change from pizza and beer, to chicken and rice and when asked that question, how many people are going to say yes to it right now?

The systems that I have used and embraced are the most successful ones that I have ever seen. I have been an open minded student of the business of fitness for over 12 years. In markets all over the world and in clubs from small to large I searched for the most successful way to make selling fitness an enjoyable experience for every person who steps foot through the door of a fitness center from the front desk person to the owner from the client to the trainer these words and systems are gold!

Chapter 19

THE WAY TO MAKE YOUR POTENTIAL CLIENTS KNOW THAT THEY DON'T KNOW

One of most common objections that you may encounter will come in varying forms. It is important to eliminate this problem before it stops you from closing a sale. In order to devise a plan of action for your member you must first get them to understand that they need your help. This is best done on the floor as the last place you want hear "I want to try it on my own" is at the table when trying to close the deal. Develop a plan of action that will make your member understand that they need your help, do this in a manner that is consistent with your approach prior to the sales process. The most important aspect of helping the guest come to the conscious realization is not an easy task. There are several steps that the member must go through in their minds in order to be fully aware that they don't know what they thought they knew.

1. The first step is the unconscious incompetence, that's where your member isn't aware of what they don't know.

2. Step number two is the conscious incompetence, that's where your member realizes what they don't know.

3. Step three is the conscious competence, that's where they have to think about it in detail before they are able to complete a set task.

4. Step number four is the unconscious competence, that's where an individual is able to perform a task with great ease and without having to think about it.

Knowing these steps to the human behavioral learning process you will begin to understand and pre-determine a set path for preparing your member's mind. I have developed a system that I use for preparing the member to understand that they need my help. The system consists of a three-step process.

Step 1: A statement of fact: *"We have 50 treadmills. The treadmills are used for cardiovascular and respiratory conditioning. They are state of the art and have springboards to protect your joints from injury."*

Step 2: The above is followed by two to three questions that will enable the guest to understand that we have information that can help them to be more successful, and to accomplish their goals faster than they would working out on their own. *"John, do you know what your target heart rate is?" "John, are you aware of the exact time, intensity, and duration that you should do cardio exercise to achieve optimal results?"*

Step 3: Step three is a tie down. A tie down is a question that invokes a "yes" response or gains agreement from the client. To help me accomplish this, I simply nod my head when I use a tie down. *"John, it sounds like you may benefit from having one of our certified professionals tell you about target heart rate."*

I use this three-step system to describe several areas of fitness or equipment in my club. It would be difficult for a guest to not know the answers to all of these questions and still say they do not need any help. Also remember that some small talk and rapport building is important during your orientation. You do not want to sound like you know it all. Telling your potential client that they need to lose weight or they need to get in shape will just invoke thoughts of doubt. I have found the art of selling personal training is based mainly on asking questions to help our guests think for themselves and make their own decisions. You stimulate their thought process through a series of questions and must remember to let the guest answer each question fully and completely before asking your next question. There is an old saying that goes, "telling is not selling." Wouldn't you agree? If you tell someone they need to lose weight or need to get started on a personal training program, they may believe you or they may doubt it. If you ask a person what brought them in today, and they say they need to lose weight, in that person's mind, it is true. The question, "What brought you in today?" stimulates people to ask themselves, "Why *did* I come to the club today?" After they answer your question, you may even want to follow up by asking, "Why do you want to lose weight?" They may answer, "My doctor told me I had to lose weight," or, "My clothes do not fit me anymore." At this point you may follow up that question by saying, "How does that make you feel?" These different questions will stimulate the guests to think on their own. It is important to let the guests make their own decisions based on their own thoughts. These thoughts can be stimulated through questions, not by statements and not by you telling them.

I have listed some questions that you can ask and the areas in which you can ask them, as well as some great tie downs to make your tours more effective. There are many ways to give a tour, and this is just one of them. It gives you the room to add your own style whereby you should try to create excitement and awe wherever possible.

Proper Food Intake

Questions

1. How important would you guess that proper food intake is for you to accomplish your fitness goals?

2. How is your food intake right now?

3. Did you know that "hunger" is actually the biggest enemy to accomplishing body fat reduction?

Tie Downs

1. Proper food intake is actually 60 to 70 percent of your success, so can you see the importance of meeting with Tom to have a meal plan strategy customized according to your lifestyle and food preferences, correct?

2. Can you see how meeting with Tom will eliminate all of your

guesswork related to food intake and accomplishing your goals? That is something you are definitely interested in, right?

Proper Cardiovascular Prescription

Questions

1. Are you aware of what your target heart rate is? Do you know why it is important?

2. Are you familiar with the Frequency, Intensity, Time, and Type (FITT) principle?

Tie Downs

1. How would you like to have a trainer show you the least amount of cardio necessary to accomplish your goals?

2. Isn't it nice that we have trainers to eliminate your guesswork and design the most effective program for you?

Proper Supplementation

Questions

1. Did you know that if you are exercising and you are not supplementing, your metabolism is probably not functioning optimally?

2. Did you know that it is well documented that if you were to get all of the nutrients your body needs to truly be functioning at its best from food alone that you would have to eat more than 4,500 calories a day? How close do you think you would get to your goal of eating 4,500 calories a day?

Tie Downs

1. There are a lot of products here that do a lot of different things. Fortunately you do not need to take all of them, right? And even more fortunate, isn't it nice to have a fitness professional that will educate you so you do not have to figure it out all by yourself?

2. Aren't you glad that you can work with a fitness professional to eliminate all of your guesswork when it comes to supplementation?

Proper Resistance Training

Questions

1. Are you aware of why resistance training is important for someone with your goals of reducing body fat?

2. What have you done for resistance training in the past? Do you feel that what you have done has given you the best possible results?

Tie Downs

1. How would you like to work with a trainer and get set up with the ideal number of sets, reps, and rest periods, and which exercises are best for achieving your goals?

2. Does it make sense that if you are going to be completely set up for success you would want to have a certified trainer to personally customize your program to suit your individual needs?

Again, these are just suggestions. You are free to include some questions of your own. These questions and tie downs have been tried and tested for many years and have been met with outstanding results.

Chapter 20

TIME MANAGEMENT

Effective time management is imperative in order to lead a successful life. Everyone from students, to housewives, to the CEO must have a structured system that creates good habits. I cannot stress enough the impact effective time management can have on your success in life. You only have so much time and when that time is up, your life is over. For many of us procrastination takes over, bad habits are formed and we never accomplish the things we want in life because we do not have good time management skills.

One of the owners that I used to work for was always quick to bring up a story about his ditch digging theory. He would say that one of his employees would spend all day digging a ditch. It was deep, long and faultlessly round. It was a perfect ditch. He worked hard all day and he was happy with his accomplishment. When he was finished, he would come back into the club and say, "I worked hard all day. I even have blisters on my hands and now I am finally done. Isn't it a beautiful ditch?" And the owner would reply, "Yes, you have worked hard and indeed it is a beautiful ditch. There is only one problem, we don't need a ditch!"

There are two ways to work. You can work hard or you can work smart. I found the later to be much more lucrative.

The story is to remind you that your job is to sell personal training and get members results. It is important to keep *the main thing, the main thing.* Work smart, not hard, and stay focused on the business at hand. If your club is like mine, you only get paid for selling and completing sessions. Do you realize that if you spend 10 minutes a day saving money, 10 minutes a day learning a foreign language, 10 minutes a day writing a book and 10 minutes a day on building a house that in a couple of years, you would have saved a lot of money, you would speak a foreign language, would have written a book and even built a house all in under 40 minutes a day. I relate time management to the prospective client sitting across from you during a sale. Every day you know you should do these things, but every day your mind tricks your body into "thinking about it," trying it out, into putting it off until the next day. That "other day" will never come. You will be an old person sitting around telling yourself, "I should have, I could have, if only..." My mentor taught me one of the most valuable lessons I have ever learned in this business. He said to me, "Have a five-year plan, have a one-year plan, have a monthly plan and have a daily plan." Looking back on this advice now, I did not always hit my daily plan. But I came pretty close. I did not always hit my monthly plan, but I came pretty close. I did not always hit my annual plan, but I would come pretty close. I think you know the answer to the five-year plan. Achieving small goals is the foundation the reaching large ones. Take baby steps. No step is too small, and no goal or dream is too big. If you have a plan and manage your time then your dream can be accomplished.

My whole system is based on accountability and time management. The system can only work if you use it, and you can only use it if you manage your time correctly. Sit down with your manager or mentor and put together your goals. Once you have done that, work toward devising a plan in order to achieve those goals. In the end, anything can be achieved.

What I Should Do When I Get to Work

1. Walk through the club. (Meet and greet members and check equipment for maintenance and cleanliness.)

2. Confirm personal training appointments and orientations.

3. Update your statistics and personal planner.

4. Update and check the Master Training Appointment Book.

5. Check and call all new membership agreements from the previous day and make orientation appointments and use welcome greetings.

6. Schedule at least three orientation appointments.

7. Sit in on three new membership presentations.

8. Workout with one other personal trainer and compare techniques, role-play on sales presentations.

9. Check-out with your fitness supervisor and make sure your goals are achieved.

Chapter 21

P.T. RE-SIGNS

Re-signing a personal training client can be just as important as signing a new one. Not only is it important in helping your members to accomplish their goals, but also crucial in maintaining a steady income. Many of the successful trainers that have had long-term success do so through a steady and reliable source of re-signing clients. It is important to remember that many exercise enthusiasts prefer to exercise only when they have a personal trainer present. Developing a consistent system for re-signing clients will ensure a quality recurring personal training business.

Having good long-term success as a personal trainer can be very rewarding. This can only happen if you are able to maintain a healthy relationship with your occupation. You should get along with your clients, that is, if you're forced to train people that you are not comfortable with, you may find that your job is intolerable. Loving what you do, or dreading the mere fact of even showing up to work, could all depend on picking and choosing a quality group of clients that you yourself feel comfortable with. Once you have established a quality group of clients, you may then begin to determine your hours, your number of clients, and even the rates you charge. These benefits may only be enjoyed if you are able to maintain and re-sign a quality client list.

I will give you several presentations that will help in your ability to re-sign a quality client list.

"Mary, I couldn't help but notice that you only have 3 sessions of personal training left. I'm also sure that you are aware that tomorrow is the final day for our closeout special. We have had incredible success together and I think you would agree that we want to continue in accomplishing all of our original goals. Your success is my success. I would recommend that you reserve your 8:30 time slot before one of my other clients tries to take it."

A personal trainer has the unique ability to work with their clients on a daily basis, sometimes using a take-away close can help to set your self up for future success.

"Mary, I know that this may be an uncomfortable question, and I know that you like to work out after you get off work at 6pm. I have a VIP client who is interested in working out and retaining my services. If you are not interested in re-signing on a long-term package, I may have to reserve this time slot for another individual."

As you begin to evolve as a personal trainer and as a sale person you will start to realize that the two things are not separate, they are one in the same. In the beginning, it is important to focus on each separate area, but as you become more experienced, you may start to realize that selling is part of the job. My personal training re-sign presentation has evolved so far that I don't even give my clients an option.

"Mary, as my client, you agreed that you would put a 100% effort in accomplishing your goal. As your personal trainer, I feel that it is my job to give you no other option than accomplishing your original goal. I have already filled out your agreement for another 20 sessions, this was a special package price that our club offered, and I told my boss to reserve 20 sessions at the discounted rate. Mary, do you want to handle your package by cash or credit card."

It is impossible to get your clients results if you cannot get them to complete their training. The most important thing to remember in re-signing your clients is that you cannot wait until they finish their entire package, if you wait till the last session, you will have little success in re-signing. You should start selling personal training when your client has 3-4 sessions left.

Chapter 22

WORKING THE FLOOR

The beauty of working in a health club can come from many different aspects in our business. If you are selling anything from cars to copy machines to health club memberships, the hardest thing about the job is getting the people in front of you. When I refer to the beauty of our business, I am referring to the fact there is a steady stream of customers flowing into our facility at any given moment. I see many membership representatives or personal trainers, who think that the only way to make a living is to wait for walk-ins or wait for their orientation appointments to show up. The truth of the matter is evident that all the business you will ever need to make a substantial income is right in front of your eyes. If you have ever worked in a club that does very little advertising or has very little walk in traffic you would have had to rely on other avenues to create your income. There are some very simple rules that can make a difference in your ability to work the floor. Follow these rules and you will never have to worry about walk-ins or waiting for the guests to come to you.

Rule 1:

For the majority of the members that are working out in your particular facility image is everything. Most of our members will not admit that they need help. It is important to understand that your members may not understand how to get results or even how to do basic exercises. This absence of knowledge may create shortcomings in your members' abilities to get results, as most members will not ask for help. You must understand that this gap exists.

Rule 2:

Although it is important to contact your members, it is also very important to make sure you are not intrusive. One common complaint that I hear from members that work out in health clubs is that they feel the trainers tend to be overly aggressive. When I approach a member on the work out floor, I never linger. I may say something like "I noticed your technique and I though I might be able to offer some pointers. My desk is right over here. And if you like, stop by to see me after your work out."

Rule 3:

This rule has made a substantial increase in my ability to add creditability to my knowledge. I have a detailed filing system of articles that pertain to all aspects of health and fitness. These articles may vary from a wide range of different topics on anything from medical conditions, to how to exercise properly. I have articles from supplementation to injury rehabilitation. It is important in any type of sale to give before you get. I may offer to make copies of the article for the member, the web sites for club business or fitness management magazines which offer years of back issues and have detailed articles for the purpose of education.

Rule 4:

It is important to remember that you can offer a quick session. This would include going out on the workout floor, offering a short session for no cost. The best time to go out on a work out floor and offer some pointers would be NOW! Don't be afraid or hesitate when it comes to taking your member through a quick work out based on education, giving your member the service that they came to a fitness center for.

Rule 5:

Although most trainers spend a substantial amount of time on the education and on the exercise knowledge, most trainers will fall short when it comes to producing an income. Asking for money is part of being a personal trainer. If you cannot get a member to enroll into a personal training package, you will have very little success in helping your members get results. It is important to practice the use of high quality presentations such as those mentioned in previous chapters, that have been tested and tried and have been proven to be successful. You should have these presentations memorized word for word and you cannot be afraid of offering your service for a fee. Most of the problems caused in regards to the selling process come from the guest feeling pressured from an untrained, unprofessional trainer using a broken selling system. The trainer may be feeling the same pressure from not memorizing this kind presentation, thus not being prepared. Practice makes perfect!

Rule 6:

You must offer personal training sitting down. I cannot give you a detailed explanation of why it is important to present personal training sitting down. But your odds of closing a sale increase substantially once you are sitting at the table.

Rule 7:

The last and most important step that many personal trainers fail to adhere to is the good old fashion art of asking for a T/O (take over). Don't be afraid to ask for help. You may just learn something!

Working the floor for personal training can be a rewarding avenue for a higher income and increasing your client base. This endless source of people can be tapped into if you practice the steps that I have outlined above. Remember as a quality instructor you must have the ability to recruit and keep quality clients, selling is part of your job!

Chapter 23

THE WALL OF FAME

I am sure if you have spent enough time to get to this point in the book, then you are probably like me. You are one of those individuals who spend a substantial amount of time on developing your education level. A good percentage of your time is probably spent studying written material, magazines or articles or just plain learning from other successful companies in our industry. One of the most successful authors in terms of fitness and their impact on the health club business would be Bill Phillips of EAS. He developed the book "Body for Life." This incredible fitness system was on the New York Times bestseller list for more than a year. Another company that has been extremely successful in terms of their sales and production would be Weight Watchers. As a student dedicated to improving our ability to recruit, sell and get results for personal training clients, we have found that one thing these two companies use in a very successful manner would be the before and after concept. This successful concept was used everywhere in the 70s and 80s and really seem to die out during the 90s. But now if you look at these types of sales or marketing techniques, you can see that many companies are going back to this proven success method for promoting their product. In my clubs I set up a wall of fame. The wall should have lots of pictures; they should be before and after shots. With today's digital cameras this should be a cinch. The next step is the testimonial. This should come in the form of a letter and, the member should write it. It should outline the steps that were taken in order to gain success with the one-on-one personal training program.

- **What package did they buy?** This is important because it gives the potential client some insight into what needs to be done in terms of investment and may relieve some of the anxiety about what package to get started on!

• **How many times a week did they work with the trainer?** Working with a trainer requires a bit of re-allocation and life style adjustment. The wall may relieve some of those concerns as well. It may also give your potential client expectations of commitment

• **How long were the workouts and what did they consist of?** The workout routine is very important because seeing the progress and the routine helps the members see the amount of time and planning that goes into the sometimes complex art of getting your members results

• **What supplements did they take and what was the food intake like?** Supplements and meal replacements have become commonplace in most training programs and if they are not adjusted properly the results may be slow coming.

• **How many days off did you have?** This will be vital to many of your members and the days off may be a necessity. Make sure to show that all of your clients may have had a day or even weeks off at some point in the quest for success and these set backs don't stop success. This shows the reality of the program and highlights your compassion to your potential client.

• **What was the role of the trainer?** This is the most important part of the wall of fame. You have to explain the role of the trainer and how the trainer made a difference in the success of the program. For example, Mary stated that she had tried many different programs and this was the first time she had any type of long term success, therefore the trainer was the difference.

• **When did you first start to see results?** For many of the new personal training clients the first sign of change is very slow and sometimes weight loss may take two or three weeks before any substantial changes occur. Again it is important to show new clients that they are not alone in this battle and that the successful clients had the same slow start. This is just part of the battle and if others have done it so can they.

• **Show the before and after measurements?** Show the numbers. This is concrete evidence of individual achievements. If you do a good job on the orientation you should have an outline of the before measurements, the body fat percentage, weight, and so on If it is in black and white your clients can visualize their progress and feel proud.

• **And be sure to include the obvious, how do you feel now?** It is also good to let the potential clients know that once goals have been reached with the assistance of a personal trainer one experiences physical rewards. This is important. The feeling of success is something everyone can relate to and should be instilled with a plaque on the wall of fame.

The wall of fame should be put in a high profile place near the personal training area and should be updated often. The message should be perfectly clear; if you want to be successful you should do what every one else is doing! If you want to be successful; get a personal trainer!

CHAPTER 24

THE CLOSEOUT MASTER PLAN

As the ultimate personal trainer, it is important to use all of the resources possible to develop and enhance your ability to recruit and involve clients in the program. The closeout master plan is a detailed outline of what it would take for you to develop an incredible buying frenzy. In this day and age, most health clubs are familiar with a closeout party but there are still many clubs that do not believe in having this type of promotional event. In the twelve years that I have worked in the health club business, I have never seen a club use a properly developed closeout system and not produce a positive response from the clients, employees and members. As a personal trainer this is a checklist of sorts that you should have in your daily planner. You can go over it starting a couple days before the closeout party to make sure you are successful. One good closeout should represent about five days worth of revenue. One bad closeout is equal to five bad days. Be aware of this and make sure that you are set up and ready. Remember, health clubs are about energy. The best operators are the ones that can create the energy, not only among the members and guests, but also among the staff. "Macy's white flower day," if you can tell me what a white flower day is, you are smarter than me. The most successful day in retail store sales for many years was a closeout created by Macy's Department Store. It has nothing to do with anything other than a sale and the energy created by it.

A closeout in short is a party! A huge fiesta put together to create a buying frenzy. Most health clubs will do the majority of the work for you and in mentioning work I am referring to the little things done by your club that build up the hype. It is still important to understand the process and do your part. All of the clubs passes (three and ten days) will expire or be extended on that day. All corporate open enrollment periods should be expiring that day. All special pricing will be expiring that day. One hundred "hot colored signs will be up in the club, announcements are being made every 10 minutes, the telephone is answered in a different way and all schedules are cleared of member problems, personal training sessions or nutrition sessions. Closeout is set up for selling only. Post-dated checks or credit cards should all be made for the 15th or the 30th of the month; this creates excitement among the staff. The contests box for the trip give-a-way should be front and center: The most important part about the trip give-a-way or the raffle is that you must be present to win. Also think about making a rule "bringing in a non-member is the only way to enter." The two most important elements of the party are the "raffle" in the evening or throughout the day and having several "outside vendors" coming in to promote their product. This will create a festive atmosphere in your club. Make sure that all staff is at the club by 8:00 a.m. And that the club is decorated by 9:00 a.m. Make sure to have one person scheduled to come in extremely early because there is a whole group of members and guests that like to come in early and you may miss an opportunity. You may be able to upgrade a membership or sell some personal training. The person that wants to make the biggest paycheck is probably the person that will be there early.

The Set Up

1. As you can see from the things I have listed above, the closeout set up starts from the beginning of the month. Developing good habits will ensure your success by following the points outlined above on a daily basis. The most important aspect of your personal performance on closeout will come from your ability to

clear your schedule and book only handpicked orientation or sales opportunities. I like to hand pick my closeout orientations and I do this by having a free body fat testing booth set up a couple days prior to the party. I hand pick potential clients that seem interested. If they seem like they are interested in a one on one session, I book them for an appointment during our closeout party.

2. Each personal trainer or membership counselor should have a job assignment for the party. An example would be making a trainer in charge of setting up and running a supplement booth. Someone else may be in charge of making sure the club is decorated with balloons. Another example would be to have one trainer in charge of enrolling vendors to make the event more festive. The key to success will come from your team working from a plan.

3. Each trainer should have approximately 15 orientations set. Those appointments should consist of 30 minute time periods and a goal for production should be set. These appointments should be confirmed and the confirmation call should include a brief explanation outlining the day's events.

4. Each trainer should call 50 current members and 50 missed guests to promote the closeout party. Call and leave messages and tell your potential clients and members about the opportunities, giveaways or even invite them to bring friends and families to workout free of charge.

5. Signs must be up and the trainers, counselors, the front desk staff and even the janitors should know the promotion. Have it planned and be sure to send out several confirmation calls. Have a production with the staff or be involved in one so that every individual in the company is aware of the promotion and what the signs mean.

6. All "balance dues" and "promise to pays" must be collected or scheduled for closeout. Everyone that owes money should be called and told to come in on closeout to pay their balance or they will be sent to collections.

7. Advise the front desk of telephone salutations and start it to-day. "Thank you for calling _____on our closeout sale, how may I help you?" Promote whatever the special is when giving the telephone salutation and attach a copy of it to the telephone.

8. One counselor should be working the front desk all day for "flips" and renewals. Make sure that one person is at the desk working check-ins and making sure that every person that walks in is told about the specials. This is a huge source of revenue for the company.

9. Before counselors go home make sure that all appointments are written in the master appointment book.

10. All post dates should be put on the books and make sure to write them down the night before closeout. This way you know exactly how much needs to be made in order to hit your goal.

11. Spread the hype with each and every employee about the big day that is happening tomorrow. Make sure that everyone knows and understands what closeout is.

12. The front desk should have a retail or sidewalk sale set up and they should handle any food, fashion shows or sidewalk sales. Trainers should be doing orientations, potential sales only and be in charge of supplement or personal training seminars in the aerobics room. Nutritionists should clear their schedules and be in charge of vitamin seminars or nutrition seminars. Aerobics instructors should do a dance seminar at some point in the evening or a spinning demonstration out in front of the club.

13. Closeout should not cost the company money and should be part of the employee's job description. The staff will be getting paid extra commission based on the extra sales made. All trips, food and vendors should be traded out with the approval of the general manager or regional manager. No trade outs can be accepted for personal or staff use.

On the Day of Closeout

On the day of closeout you should have this list posted in your office and in your planner and you should make sure to do everything on the list.

1. On closeout, have a morning production meeting and motivate everybody. Get them excited. Let everyone know what is riding on the clubs performance by highlighting where the club is at and what needs to be done in order to hit your goals.

2. Get balloons, streamers, and signs up so the club looks like there is a party going on.

3. Don't deal with any cancellations or customer service issues today. Today is pure production. No negativity is allowed.

4. Do 25 percent off retail and supplements and set up booths for the promotion of this such as, 'buy 2 get the 3rd one free' or 'buy 1 and get the 2nd for 50 percent off.'

5. Continue to promote the evening over the telephone.

6. No workouts for employees allowed on closeout.

7. Emphasize paid in full options. Every package should offer 1, 3 or 5 sessions free.

8. Make sure you have something to give-a-way to members. Do trade-outs with businesses to give away in a drawing on closeout. This creates a buying atmosphere.

9. Have an afternoon production meeting.

10. Nobody "walks" on closeout. Call your district manager to approve deals.

11. Dress in a different or new uniform. In my clubs I like to have a theme this gives the staff a chance to wear apparel of their choosing that coincides with the theme. Appearance and presence are half the battle.

Chapter 25

SELLING SUPPLEMENTATION

When I first started in the health club business, most clubs had not yet developed a game plan for promoting supplements; in fact in the early 90's many did not offer supplements as part of their retail centers. The art of selling supplements to our members is something that is still being developed. There are several effective ways to market our pro shop products.

There have been many debates as to whether or not supplements are good for you. Most health club supplements are not approved by the F.D.A. this means that they are not required to have specific regulations or ingredients. The lack of regulation for these kinds of products can vary drastically, and long-term effects have yet to be determined. It is important when offering these products that you do not tell your members and guests that they need to take a certain supplement or drug. I always try to prescribe supplements in a manner that is consistent with feedback from other people that have used the products. For example, "we have several members who have taken this product and have seen substantial changes in their bodies during the time they were using this supplement." Health clubs have come under scrutiny and have had some law suits associated with trainers telling members that they wouldn't get results if they didn't take a certain vitamin.

Offering supplementation in your retail center can vary in volume from club to club. One club may sell one jug of protein a week whereas another may sell one hundred. I have worked in high volume retail clubs and selling vitamins will be much easer if you follow a few simple steps

• One of two things must happen! Either the club should offer the vitamins the trainers are taking, or the trainers are required to take the supplements the club is selling. You guys can figure out the details, but the bottom line is if the staff is using a certain product this will make it sensationally more desirable. The rule to consume and sell the products from your club.

• Put the product in the consumer's hand. Once the product is in the person's hand they will be more likely to show interest. You may then answer questions as you point to the label.

• Know the current discounts- if you know the current promotions you will have more success and you may entice more of your members to show interest.

• Know your products or find someone that does.

• Attractive display- move the supplements often and use big signs.

• Offer discounts for employees and if you can, have a credit account or V.I.P. discount card.

• Put up signs on all of the cardio equipment.

• Offer drinks with scoops of supplements if you have a juice bar.

• Supplement tables or seminars.

• Use before and after pictures include the list of supplements for the individuals.

• Set up the body for life fitness challenge. A before and after E.A.S. style contest. Bill Phillips wrote the supplement guide in the mid 90s and has sold more vitamins because of it than any one I can think of.

• Most important is to know your stuff. If you don't know the latest info on any of the particular items at your club find somebody that does! Don't play the guessing game!

Following some of these simple guidelines will help you and the other members of the personal training team move supplement products.

Chapter 26

INTERACTING WITH THE STAFF

Staff interaction is an overlooked yet vital aspect of our business. Many personal trainers and sales consultants fail to do the groundwork and are unable to interact well with others. Loving your job or dreading the thought of even showing up to work could all depend on how well you work with your surrounding staff. Since we are in a commission driven business, trainers can become competitive. At times will even cross the line of stealing or "sharking" packages. The way to handle these problems is quickly, privately and usually through your manager or fitness supervisor. Problems that are not handled immediately can fester into much larger problems that can affect the entire club.

Your manager

You club manager or fitness supervisor is the person who has the most to gain from your success in the club. At this level I can almost guarantee the managers are tied in to a piece of everything you sell, they truly have a vested interest in making sure that you are successful. I have found that many trainers being part time or being scheduled to work hours that do not always coincide with the management often become alienated from the people that are the true professionals in the club. Spend as much time as you can in an attempt to find out how these individuals think and what they want. Being in tune with the wants and needs of the person that hands out your pay check will increase your ability to grow and to learn from someone who has a proven track record in the industry. It is also important to understand that whenever there is a problem that concerns a new or important client, the manager is the one who will deal with it. In many cases these clients have had problems or need a new trainer. Since they have usually spent (or spend) a lot of money on training the manager will only hand out these clients to the trainers that they trust or have a good reputation for understanding the company systems.

Front desk

One time I was upset because one of my important clients scheduled an early morning appointment on my day off of all things. I canceled a trip to meet with them and drove all the way to the club early in the morning to find that the front desk person had not written down the message. My client had canceled the appointment many days prior. Being in the bad mood from the early wake up call I let this individual have it! Things really got ugly at that point and not only did I stop getting my messages but I found that my orientations were all kids with no money and people that had no interest in buying personal training. What I found is that these people actually recommend trainers to many of the members. I found that many of the potential clients interested in having a one on one personal trainer would first ask the service desk staff which person they felt was the best trainer.

Other trainers

Many of the trainers in the health club business today have a lot of knowledge on different aspects of exercise. It has been through the relationships that I have built in the business that I have been able to keep my knowledge and skills sharp. I spend 2 hours a week making sure that I squeeze in a workout with one of the other trainers. Ask questions, workout together, trade clients, do sales role-playing and rely on them as sales professionals. This trainer can answer a question about an area that is their specialty; this resource is at your fingertips. Use it and build a good relationship with your teammates.

Mentor

Not everyone starts off with great instincts when it comes to being a trainer or the related sales process, but whatever abilities people have can be nurtured and developed. My first six months in a role where I was forced to sell personal training were very difficult. I felt that I was good with people but I did not have much in the way of natural sales ability. The system that I put together is geared towards people like myself: the 99 percent that are not gifted in sales. I feel that anyone can sell a package if they have the determination and ability to learn the system. There was no system when I started; it was just my mentor and I. He showed me his methods, he critiqued my weak points, gave me encouragement, TOed for me, helped me to understand the rules of the game and showed me the correct way to fill out a personal training agreement.

I owe most of my early success to my mentor. I probably would not have lasted as a trainer if I hadn't had someone like this to help me. What did he gain in return? That is a simple answer. I worked on his team. If he needed to have someone to stay late, or come in early, I was there. If he needed someone to work on Sunday, I was there. When he became a supervisor, I followed him to every club that he worked in. I followed out every task he asked down to the smallest detail. When he became a district director, he promoted me to a manager and sent me to any club that was doing poorly. I followed the system and increased sales in the low clubs so that they became the top clubs. Our relationship helped our company become more successful, and, in turn, we helped each other in becoming more successful. We made more money, because we worked together.

Sales

These are the guys you want to get in good with. In most cases the sale people in the club have access to the new members. The people that have just signed up are the best source of new clients. Building a good relationship with the sales department will put you in an ideal position to pick and choose the orientations that you feel have some interest in training or have some interest in you as their trainer. As you build this symbolic relationship you may even find yourself being brought in to the sales process to T.O. for training or you may ask the help of the sales department for some help closing one of your clients! It is important to send any new sign ups for memberships to the sales person that is helping you and you will see a huge improvement in you training schedule

Increase Your Sales Knowledge

As the complete professional, you must continue to grow. You must improve your knowledge, your sales skills and your training information. Our business is a rapidly changing one. If you do not continue to grow, you will be left in the dust. The young people just starting in our business are at the top of their game. They are top athletes trained by the latest technology, and they know there is money to be made in our industry. They are hungry. There is a poster above my desk and it says, *"Every morning on the planes of Africa, the lion awakes, and knows it must outrun the slowest gazelle or it will starve to death. Every morning on the same plane, the gazelle awakes and knows it must outrun the fastest lion, or it will be killed." It does not matter if you are the lion or the gazelle. When you wake up in the morning, you'd better be running."*

We work in the one of the fastest growing industries in the world. Computerization has changed the amount of energy that we expel at work. By the year 2010, 25 percent of all Americans will be working from their homes. You literally will not even have to get up and walk in order to accomplish your job. The obesity rate is reaching staggering heights and the amount of information available about fitness grows every day. Doctors are getting smarter, nutritionists are getter better, and supplementation has improved. Lets face it; fitness centers have come a long way from the old strap machine that jiggles your fat away (by the way, there was still one of those in the first gym that I worked).

Commissions.

The rules for splits and commissions can be at the forefront of many of the staff problems that arise in a health club. It is important to lay down the ground rules for how to handle these sensitive issues. I suggest posting the rules so that every one is clear on how splits and other commissions work.

The interaction between sales and trainer can be a fine line of controversy so the rule that we have used for splits is the following. A T.O. should never be split. If a trainer conducts a T.O. for a sales person or a sales person does a T.O. for a trainer, the original person should receive all the commission. New trainers will not T.O. if they have to split their deals. (A supervisor or manager should generally do a T.O.) If a trainer has an appointment for a membership, it is an appointment and should be split with the trainer. The trainer must have the appointment in the book or in their planner. If you have a person come back to the club, and it is not in the MAB and they do not ask for you, it is not yours. If a walk in asks for someone one it is an ask-for or an appointment and should be split if it is taken by some one other than the requested person. If a sales person sells a package that commission goes entirely to the sales person. A package sold by the sales department should be given to the fitness director for trainer allocation. The sales staff counselor can only sign up a member on a training package if; #1 The member has never bought P.T. #2 The member has a package that has been expired for more than a month. #3 At the point of sale on a new membership. Trainers should let the members know that if they are interested in any fitness programs they should go through them and can specify that this is how they earn a living. Last but not least, orientations go to the trainer.

These are just some of the rules we run at our clubs. We have used these rules for years, and they work very well. Remember, what goes around comes around. If you are not consistent, you will run into problems in which case remember to handle your issues immediately and fairly. You may even consider posting the rules, so that everybody is clear on them. In one of the clubs I worked in, the manager had the sales staffs vote on each rule, he then posted the rules on the wall and we never had a problem.

Negativity is the cancer that ruins your paycheck. Do not get caught up in other people's business. Mom always says, "Mind your own business." Remember, if you have complaints or something negative to say, complaints go up. Complaints don't go level or down, they go up. Keep focused on your business at hand, stay away from the fun bunch and have clear rules of commission. Stay on the good side of all the departments, attend meetings, and follow your to-do list every single day. By following simple rules of staff interaction, you will truly love your job in the fitness industry.

Chapter 27

GIVING A FREE GIFT WITH PURCHASE

I don't know why, but the old free gift with purchase gets them every time, just ask the department stores. They have made millions of dollars in their cosmetic departments just by offering a free gift along with a purchase of a package. I have had good success with three different options in reference to a free gift with purchase.

1. The first option that has worked well for our company has also been used to generate interest in almost all of the companies that I have worked for. It is a very simple process, basically if a member enrolls in the starter package, they will receive a limited time prize. For instance, "enroll in the starter package between now and the end of the month and receive a free Sony Walkman. This offer expires 11/30/2004." You can do the same for the accelerated result package. Get started on the accelerated result package between now and the end of the month and receive a free LV wallet. When I use the free gift with purchase program, I only use the item available for about a five-day period and I rarely use the same item twice. Many of these items may be purchased for a discount or a partial trade for a membership. Remember to ensure your manager has approved all trade outs!

2. The second option has also been used to provide outstanding results and to create urgency at the end of the month. The process for offering the free gift with purchase comes in the form of a larger prize and depending on the amount of sessions that you purchase, you will receive one entry for each session. So for example, a client enrolls in the starter package and receives six entries whereas a client that purchases 32 sessions would have 32 entries in the drawing. Once again to create urgency, the drawing is held on closeout and the only people who are invited to participate in this drawing are those who enrolled in the one on one program during the competition dates.

3. The third option is where you have a contest or a challenge that includes a set amount of sessions and a prize for the winner of the challenge. So for instance, the program may require each contestant to complete 32 sessions of personal training in a 60-day period. Based on the evaluation results taken at the end of the 60-day period prizes can be given to the top three contestants. As an extra incentive you may wish to offer a free T-shirt to anyone who participates.

Chapter 28

CONFIRMING APPOINTMENTS AND CANCELLATIONS

If you have been a trainer for any period of time, you will find yourself in situations where you have the devil on your left shoulder and an angel on your right shoulder. You will be sitting in front of a check with your name on it and a client who is happy to deliver another large package. As you wipe the beads of sweat from your forehead, the words are going through your mind, "Should I or shouldn't I?" Another twenty hours spent in anguish over a client who takes advantage of my generosity and hard work. We talked earlier about the difference between loving your day-to-day life as a career personal trainer and dreading the next reenrollment. It all depends on your ability to keep a healthy relationship with your trade and your client base. Loving your job or dreading the thought of even showing up to work can all depend on how well you establish boundaries with your clients. When it comes to rescheduling and cancellation of appointments, I try to set down the rules for what is and is not acceptable and what it will cost per session. On the following page are some of the rules we run at our clubs. We have used these rules for years and they have worked very well for us. If you do not practice consistency it is likely that you will run into problems.

Always remember to handle your issues immediately and consistently. You may even consider posting the rules, so that everybody is clear on them. You can also have your clients sign a waiver that has all the rules listed so that there are no misunderstandings and then post the rules on the wall. We never had problems in the past when doing this as the client is left unable to feign ignorance. The confirmation box will allow you make a note if the appointment has been confirmed. I like to call my appointments from home just to confirm that they are coming in before I leave for the club. Also, it is important to call and check the book to see if any new appointments have been scheduled for the day. Your personal training clients should have access to your voicemail system so they can call if they have any last minute cancellations.

One of the most important relationships you can have will be with your front desk staff, as they are the first contact. They can control your paycheck.

Agreement for personal training guidelines

1. All personal training sessions must be made or rescheduled 24 hours prior to the appointment time. Training sessions that are not cancelled in advance may still incur a charge. All clients are responsible for having the direct phone line or message center to their particular trainer. Messages left at the front desk or at the corporate office may not reach trainer in time to be considered 24 hour advanced notice.

2. #1 Fitness personal trainers have hourly personal training appointments. Please be aware that if you are late, irrespective of your session start time, your trainer must finish on time and not run over.

3. As a #1 Fitness member, you agree to the time limit in which the personal training package must be completed. If extra time is required to complete the package, this extension must be approved by the #1 Fitness corporate office.

4. All personal training clients must agree to a physical examination prior to starting a one on one personal training program. The client is responsible for making sure they are physically fit to exercise.

5. #1 Fitness has agreed to provide a trainer for the sessions indicated. #1 Fitness does not agree to make all of your sessions completed with the same trainer.

6. The client agrees to notify #1 Fitness if at any time they are not comfortable with the personal trainer they are working with. Clients may change trainers at any time. The client also agrees to notify #1 Fitness of any extended leave.

Client: _____ Trainer: _____

Chapter 29

DRILLING

Drilling is an essential part of the human behavioral learning process. Repetition is the key to perfection. Every time we do something we get a little better at it and it gradually becomes easier and easier until we reach a point where we can do it without thinking, this is the place that we long to be. **The unconscious competence: You don't have to think about riding a bike, and you don't have to think about catching a ball. You don't have to think about walking. But all of these things at one point in our life were difficult. It took a lot of effort and practice to perfect these simple things. Selling is just as easy as riding a bike, although it may not seem so to a beginner. Most people at the age of five learn to ride a bike. They don't learn to sell. A professional football player practices throwing a football every day of his life and still continues to practice every day once he gets in the pros. All-professional's drill: boxers, basketball players, racecar drivers, doctors and lawyers. Practice, practice, practice, drill, drill, drill.**

Mirroring and Matching Drill

This drill requires two personal trainers sitting face to face mirroring and matching every movement. You want to focus on the energy, the breathing, everything involved in mimicking the person to a "T".

The Question Game

The question game is a simple but effective way to learn the art of selling. This technique has been instrumental in my ability to train top-notch personal training sales professionals. Answering a question with a question and staying calm under fire is at the heart of what selling is all about. It took me a long time to develop a drill that could teach the fundamentals that were the real difference between a new sales person and a seasoned one. One day it dawned on me that the difference between a new sales person and a seasoned was as simple as the experienced sales person knowing how to ask questions instead of answering them. This is the little or **big** difference in communication styles! This drill helped put the sales person in control of the conversation thus enabling them to control the thoughts of the guest through a series of questions. When each of the questions is asked the guest needs time to think of the answer and the sales process begins. This drill is my invention and I have never seen it used in any other publication. To perform the drill sit across from another trainer and ask them a question. The other trainer (in a role playing manner), will then answer with a question, to which you will reply with another question and so forth.

Example;

Personal Trainer 1: How much does it cost for a membership?

Personal Trainer 2: Were you looking for a membership for yourself, a family or a couple?

Personal Trainer 1: Do you have aerobics?

Personal Trainer 2: What kind of aerobics classes are you interested in?

Personal Trainer 1: Do you have personal training?

Personal Trainer 2: Were you interested in a membership with personal training or just a membership today?

Personal Trainer 1: What time is the club the busiest?

Personal Trainer 2: What time will you be using the club most?

The Tough Customer Drill

This is a great drill for new trainers that want to become better at selling. You have to learn to be direct and to come back at your guest with the same energy they are giving you. This is not the time to back down. Your potential client is trying to take control, this is their technique. This is the time for you to take control by matching the abrasiveness brought on by the client.

Closing Drill

In a role-playing situation, try to overcome objections given by your fitness supervisor or another trainer. Ask your partner, "If I can get you a great deal on a training package, would you want to get started today?" Have your partner respond by saying, "Not today, maybe, I want to try it first, I would consider it and no." Drill on overcoming these objections. You may try "if it was $10 per session, would you be able to make a decision to get started on the program today?" Also drill on "out of the different package options, which one are you leaning towards?" Your partner would respond with the seven common objections. "I want to think about it!" "I need to speak to my spouse." "It is too much money." Use the steps outlined in overcoming objections. Practice overcoming five objections, and make sure your partner is being realistic: not too hard, and not too easy.

Filling Out the Personal Training Agreement Drill

This could be one of the most important drills. Most of the personal training deals that are lost are done so the moment the agreement comes out. Objections start to flow the moment the pen tries to touch the paper. Filling out the contract is the pivotal moment where most new personal trainers will lose their potential client or miss their sales. First try practicing by using stalling tactics. Pretend that you are a potential client and try grabbing the personal training agreement. Practice by answering questions with questions or by tapping your finger at the signature spot. You could try bringing up objections over paying with a credit card and even about payment method or type. You can also mention wanting to return at a later time to pay. If you can master through drilling, the ability to control your potential client during this most important time in the sales process, you will find this will highly increase your closing percentages.

Personal Training Presentation

Practice your P.T. presentation until you have learned it word for word. Drill on difficult, detailed questions on fitness that your guest may ask. Your presentation should sound smooth and unrehearsed. You should practice being an empathetic listener and your presentation should leave clients truly understanding the value of the program that you are offering to them. Remember; "practice makes perfect!"

Setting up a Free Session or Orientation

Repetition is the mother of learning and the father of action, which makes it the architect of accomplishment

When establishing a successful personal training program, the first step in your success will be filling up your orientation book. Having quality opportunities is the key to any successful business. Drilling on overcoming objections to the free workout is important. You will hear statements such as, "I will try it on my own," or, "I have the workout program that my coach wrote up for me in high school." You may even hear, "I don't need a trainer." Overcoming these objections will help you keep your book full and confirm future success.

Chapter 30

TO SELL OR NOT TO SELL

To sell or not to sell, that is the question. Recently, we have been hearing the faint whispers of a growing number of business professionals blaming the sales process as the smoking gun for all of the shortcomings in our industry. This negative force has been deemed the reason for some kind of slow growth. When putting some deep thought into this important issue we must look at our industry and we must look into the future as well as into the past. The first question I ask is "**what** slow growth?" The health club business next to the size of the McDonalds coke may be the fastest growing thing on the planet. Due to the present down turn in the economy most companies within our core markets failed to survive. While all the other businesses are thinking of ways to improve and enhance the sales process we are thinking of abandoning it.

The shortcomings that we have are a staple in any growing business. Ours comes not from the selling process but more from the lack of getting all of our ships to sail in the same direction. Not in the selling process but in the professional level, or lack thereof, which our industry requires for training and keeping a mature staff. Selling is a tool and nothing more "should the chef stop creating his mastery's in the kitchen because he is burned by the flame or blame the knife for a nick on the finger?"

Selling is a tool and when used properly it may be referred to as the greatest profession ever created by man! However, it is a very powerful and complicated tool, when used properly it can be extremely effective and when used carelessly it can be dangerous. Studied in depth it is as powerful and infinite as the human mind and yet it is also as basic in human nature as children's first questions. I agree our process must evolve and it will, but it must do so without abandoning the knowledge gained by our predecessors.

We must understand that we are dealing with people as our product. We sell dreams and results and sometimes failure, thus we must endeavor to understand that each and every guest is different. We must also accept that the incredible growth of our industry could be called the most explosive business invention of the century.

To those who say this industry and its systems are not extra ordinary and that growth means the abandonment of competition, victory and selling dreams, I say never.

Printed in the United Kingdom by
Lightning Source UK Ltd., Milton Keynes
138979UK00002B/123/A

9 781412 070874